The Unseen Evil

Natashia Roberts

Published by Natashia Roberts, 2024.

While every precaution has been taken in the preparation of this book, the publisher assumes no responsibility for errors or omissions, or for damages resulting from the use of the information contained herein.

THE UNSEEN EVIL

First edition. September 5, 2024.

Copyright © 2024 Natashia Roberts.

ISBN: 979-8224374656

Written by Natashia Roberts.

Table of Contents

Introduction 1

Chapter 1: Family Background 2

Chapter 3: Removal of Hanna's siblings 24

Introduction 42

Chapter 4: Conduct Disorder Explained....................66

Chapter 5: Bi Polar Explained 70

Chapter 6: ADHD Explained 73

Chapter 6: Revelations 80

Chapter 7: Failing Institutions..90

Chapter 8: Cases and Media Reports............................ 107

Chapter 9: In The Words of Robert 114

Chapter 10: Authors Note.. 122

Chapter 11: Documented Meetings................................ 124

Chapter 13: Conclusion.. 138

Chapter 14: Poems for Families 147

Dedicated to all the families who suffered thru the trauma and pain of unjust removals of their children.

Introduction

In the shadows of our society lies a system designed to protect the most vulnerable among us—our children. Yet, within this system, an unseen evil festers, causing irreparable harm to the very lives it aims to safeguard. "The Unseen Evil" delves into the harrowing reality of social services and the judicial system, where well-intentioned policies and procedures often go awry, leading to the wrongful removal of children from their families.

Through meticulous research and heart-wrenching real-life accounts, this book exposes the flaws and failures that permeate the welfare system. It sheds light on the bureaucratic oversights, misjudgments, and systemic issues that allow these injustices to persist. Families are torn apart, and the courts, meant to be the last bastion of justice, frequently fail to recognize and rectify these mistakes.

"The Unseen Evil" is not just a critique but a call to action. It urges policymakers, social workers, legal professionals, and society at large to acknowledge these grave errors and work towards a system that truly protects and serves the best interests of children and their families. This book is a testament to the resilience of those who have suffered and a beacon of hope for those fighting for change.

Notes:

This book is based on true life events, with real people. No real names was used to protect the identity of the victims and the minors. All information provided is to the best of the Authors knowledge and prove of misconduct will be included as far as possible. Take note that this is based on the South African statutory law under the Children's Justice Act, Act 38 of 2005 for the children's Act. Court case file numbers will be provided in some instances where applicable.

Chapter 1: Family Background

The mother Margaret came from a destructive family where abuse, sexual abuse, alcohol and severe poverty prevailed. She was sent to a Children's home but ran away from the children's home on numerous occasions, having sexual relations with older men at a very young age.

The father Robert came from a good home growing up mostly under the guidance of his grandparents as his mother passed away when he was a mere five years old and his father was not actively involved in his upbringing. Robert had a motorcycle accident at the age of eighteen and his right arm was amputated. He got married and had a daughter out of that marriage but unfortunately the marriage didn't last.

Robert and Margaret met at a night club one evening and that is how the relationship started. Soon Margaret would disappear without a word to Robert of her whereabouts although they were married and Margaret was pregnant.

Margaret would come back to Robert and ask forgiveness stating she just needed to get away from everything. Robert found out that when she leaves every now and again she goes and works as a prostitute and use alcohol excessively. Robert stood by Margaret despite the hurt she caused, he tried to help her by taking her for counselling and even to Pastors. He told her numerous times that she does not need that life anymore to no avail.

This behaviour of Margaret led to numerous fights and Robert eventually lost his work due to searching for Margaret on one of her runaway sprees.

Their daughter Hanna was born a beautiful little girl, but Margaret couldn't care less about the child. Robert took full responsibility for the child during Margaret's run aways. He would bath and feed the baby, change diapers, clean the home and do the dishes as well as the washing. Some family members assisted with baby sitting when Robert had to work.

Robert could not give up on Margaret he wanted his child to know her mother because he lost his own mother at a very young age, he didn't want that hurt on his baby girl. Robert endured severe neglect, rejection and humiliation but he took everything that Margaret did for the sake of his daughter. He kept on trying to change Margaret and her ways and he took her back with open arms everytime she came back, knowing she had been with other men.

Everytime she left Robert was devastated but he needed to be strong for his baby girl so he sucked it up and kept going. The leaving became more frequent and for longer periods of time and when Margaret was home she didn't want to take part in any responsibility she would sleep or play games all day long. Still Robert took care of the household and his daughter.

As anyone can imagine it was difficult for Robert and it caused the marriage to be one sided. Robert and Margaret got in numerous verbal fights where Maragaret would use vulgar words and scream.

Margaret one day then left with Hanna without telling Robert where she was going. Robert was concerned and he went to the police station to ask assistance to find his daughter. A social worker was send to assist in the matter and she gave Robert a letter that stated should Margaret leave the family home she is not allowed to take Hanna with her because her way of living is dangerous to the child. The social worker assisted Robert to get Hanna back in his care.

Chapter 2 The removal of Hanna

One day Robert received a call from a social worker who said Margaret wanted them to assist with the marriage problems and that he needed to bring Hanna to their offices so they can talk and work on a plan.

Robert went to the offices with Hanna where he was met with a whole panel of people from social services a NPO organisation. Margaret was also present in this meeting. The panel suggested that Hanna be placed in temporary Foster care so they can assist Robert and Margaret to solve their marriage problems. Everyone except Robert agreed, but they kept at it and Margaret gave permission to place Hanna in temporary Foster care.

Hanna 18 months old at the time was immediately removed from Robert, and the Foster parents was already there, as if it was pre decided this is how it's going to be. As per the children's act 38 of 2005 any removal of a minor the parents should be taken to children's court within twenty four hours, this however never happened with Hanna's case. Hanna was not in any immediate danger, she had food and clothes and was well taken care of by Robert.

"S 152: Removal of a child to

Temporary safe care

Without court order

• S 152(1): A designated social worker or police official may remove a

Child and place the child in temporary safe care without a court order

If there are reasonable grounds for believing:

(i) that the child is in need of care and

Protection; AND

(ii) that child needs immediate

Emergency protection; AND

(a) That the delay in obtaining a court

Order may jeopardise the child's safety and

Well-being; AND

(a) That the removal of the child form his or her

Home environment is the best way to secure that

Child's safety and well-being

• Section 152(2): Designated social
Worker must:
(a)Without delay but within
24 hours inform the parent, guardian
Or care-giver of the child of the
Removal of the child (if that person
Can readily be traced) (FORMS 36 & 37)
(a)Not later than the next court date
Inform the Clerk (FORM 36)
(a)Report the matter to the relevant
Provincial DSD (FORM 36 "

Three months after Hanna was removed from her parents a court order was obtained with documentation falsified as Robert signed one paper for the temporary placement but in court there was three papers presented to court, Robert never saw that documentation neither did Margaret see it. The Magistrate on the case didn't want to hear anything that Robert wanted to say she reprimanded him "MR Robert we are not going to play word games in my court." When Robert stated he never signed that documents presented.

Hanna was then placed at other Foster Care parents let's call them the Niewouds, there was also another child placed in the care of the same people.

With further investigation it was clear that social services never inspected the home of the Niewouds before placing Hanna in their care. The first time social services visited the Niewouds home was the day they took Hanna there. Regulations for Foster Parents was not followed in the case with Hanna. There was no screening done on the Niewouds.

https://helpkids.org.za/foster-care-placements/

Robert and Margaret got to see Hanna once a month under supervision from the Niewouds, they received videos but the other child was included on the videos. Robert saw in Hannas eyes that she was deeply unhappy and he told the social worker something is wrong with Hanna. The social worker ignored Robert observations and did nothing to investigate the matter.

Hanna started coming home to Robert and Margaret for weekend visits and at one such visit she told Robert that MR and MRS Niewoudt touches her inappropriately and that they show her sexual content on the television. Robert opened a case at the police station and he told the social worker about what Hanna said.

However nothing came of it and Hanna was left at the Niewoud residence. One day Robert received a call from Mrs Niewoud asking him if he knew that social services removed Hanna from their care. Mr Robert was not notified of this and tried to reach the social worker to find out where Hanna was. The social worker could not be reached for several weeks and by this time Robert was scared for his daughter as he didn't know where she was.

Robert conducted his own search for his daughter and found her at a children's home, he then found out that she was removed from the Niewouds due to molestation. With further investigation it was found that Hanna went for a psychological assessment and she told the psychologist about the molestation taking place. Not the social worker or the psychologist reported this to the police they only removed Hanna and the other girl and placed them in alternative placement. The social worker and the phycologist failed Hanna severely.

"People who MUST report suspected child abuse and/or neglect.

Section 11o(1) of the Children's Act, Act 38 of 2005 mandates the following category of professionals to report any reasonable suspicion of child abuse and neglect to the relevant authorities: correctional official, dentist, homeopath, immigration official, labour inspector, legal practitioner, medical practitioner, midwife, minister of religion, nurse, occupational therapist, physiotherapist, psychologist, religious leader, social services professional, social worker, speech therapist, teacher, traditional health practitioner, traditional leader or member of staff of volunteer worker at a partial care facility, drop-in centre or child and youth care centre.

Failure to report is a criminal offence, but more importantly it could leave a child at risk without support and services."

Hanna was in this children's home for quite a few years. She had weekend and holiday visits at her parental home where there was four other children born out of the marriage in the time Hanna was placed in Foster care and children's homes. The siblings of Hanna was left to stay in their parental home and Hanna could visit but there was always insufficient reasons given why Hanna could not be re unified with her family.

Hanna would often talk about what happens in the children's home when she visited her parents. One of the things she told her father was about a skull painted on a wall, they washed it off and painted over it but it kept surfacing.

She also told Robert about the one house father sexually misusing some of the girls. When Robert reported the incidents Hanna was called in and pressured to say that she lied.

Hanna started cutting herself and was placed on a anti psychotic called Nuzac. When Robert asked why is she cutting the social worker said that Hanna is merely trying to manipulate.

"Cutting and Self-Harm

en español: **Cortes y autolesiones**[1]
Medically reviewed by: **Leah J. Orchinik, PhD**[2]
Learn About Behavioral Health (Psychology and Psychiatry) at Nemours Children's Health[3]

1.	**https://kidshealth.org/es/parents/cutting.html**

2.	**https://www.nemours.org/find-a-doctor/14624-leah-orchinik-psychology-middletown.html**

3.	**https://www.nemours.org/services/child-psychology.html**

Most of us know about teens and cutting — how some use a sharp object like a razorblade, knife, or scissors to make marks, cuts, or scratches on their own body. But cutting is just one form of self-injury. Teens who self-injure also might burn, scratch, or hit themselves; bang their head; pull their hair; pinch their skin; pierce their skin with needles or sharp objects; or insert objects under their skin.

Self-harming is a serious issue that affects many teens. Like other risky behaviour's, it can be dangerous and habit-forming. In most cases, it is also a sign of deeper emotional distress. In some cases, peers can influence teens to experiment with it.

The topic of self-injury can be troubling for parents. It can be hard to understand why teens (or even preteens) would hurt themselves on purpose, and worrisome to think your teen — or one of their friends — could be at risk.

But parents who are aware of this important issue and understand the emotional pain it can signal are in a position **to help**[4].

About Self-Injury

People who self-injure usually start doing it during their teen years. Some continue into adulthood. In some cases, there's a family history of cutting or other self-harm.

A sense of shame and secrecy often goes along with it. Most teens who cut hide the marks and, if they're noticed, make excuses about them. Some teens, though, don't try to hide cuts and might even call attention to them.

Cutting often begins as an impulse. But many teens discover that once they start, they do it more and more, and can have trouble stopping. Many teens who self-injure report that it provides a sense of relief from deep painful emotions. Because of this, it's a behavior that tends to reinforce itself.

---

4.   https://kidshealth.org/en/parents/help-cutting.html

Cutting and other self-harm can become a teen's habitual way to respond to pressures and unbearable feelings. Many say they feel "addicted" to the behavior. Some would like to stop but don't know how or feel they can't. Other teens don't want to stop.

Most of the time, self-harm is not a suicide attempt. But it can be easy to underestimate the potential to get seriously sick or hurt through bleeding, infections, or other problems.

Why Do Teens Self-Injure?

Teens self-injure for many different reasons:

Powerful overwhelming emotions. Most teens who do it struggle with powerful emotions. To them, it might seem like the only way to express or interrupt feelings that seem too intense to endure. Emotional pain over rejection, lost or broken relationships, or deep grief can be overwhelming for some teens.

And many are dealing with emotional pain or difficult situations that no one knows about. Pressure to be perfect or to live up to impossible standards — their own or someone else's — can cause some teens unbearable pain. Some have been deeply hurt by harsh treatment or by situations that have left them feeling unsupported, powerless, unworthy, or unloved.

Some teens have experienced **trauma**[5], which can cause waves of emotional numbness called dissociation. For them, cutting and other types of self-harm can be a way to test whether they can still "feel" pain. Others describe it as a way of "waking up" from that emotional numbness.

Self-inflicted physical pain is specific and visible. For some, the physical pain can seem preferable to emotional pain. Emotional pain can feel vague and hard to pinpoint, talk about, or soothe.

When they cut or self-injure, teens say there is a sense of control and relief to see and know where the specific pain is coming from and

---

5.   https://kidshealth.org/en/parents/trauma-care.html

a sense of soothing when it stops. It can symbolize inner pain that might not have been verbalized, confided, acknowledged, or healed. And because it's self-inflicted, it is pain they control.

A sense of relief. Many teens describe the sense of relief they feel as they're cut or self-harm, which is common with compulsive behaviour's. Some people believe that endorphins might add to the relief teens describe when they self-injure. Endorphins are the "feel-good" hormones released during intense physical exertion. And they can be released during an injury.

Others believe the relief is simply a result of being distracted from painful emotions by intense physical pain and the dramatic sight of blood. Some teens say they don't feel the pain when they cut, but feel relieved because the visible results "show" emotional pain they feel.

Feeling "addicted." Cutting, especially, can be habit forming. Though it only provides temporary relief from emotional distress, the more a person cuts, the more they feel the need to do it. As with other compulsive behaviour's, the brain starts to connect the injury to the momentary sense of relief from bad feelings.

Whenever the tension builds, the brain craves that relief and drives the teen to seek relief again by self-injuring. So it can become a habit someone feels powerless to stop. The urge to cut — to get relief — can seem too hard to resist when emotional pressure is high.

Other mental health conditions. Self-harm is often linked to — or part of — another mental health condition. Some teens are also struggling with other urges, obsessions, or compulsive behaviour's. For some, **depression**[6] or bipolar disorder can contribute to overwhelming moods that might be hard for them to regulate. For others, mental health conditions that affect personality can cause relationships to feel intense and consuming, but unsteady. For these teens, intense positive attachments can suddenly become terribly disappointing and leave them feeling hurt, anger, or despair too strong to cope with.

---

6.   https://kidshealth.org/en/parents/understanding-depression.html

Other teens struggle with personality traits that attract them to the dangerous excitement of risky behavior or self-destructive acts. Some are prone to dramatic ways of getting reassurance that they are loved and cared about. For others, **posttraumatic stress**[7] has had an effect on their ability to cope. Or they're struggling with alcohol or substance problems."

Hanna never received any trauma counselling for the molestation, the removal from her parental home or the abuse she endured. Hanna got a ear infection, the nurse at the children's home just placed cotton wool in her ears with ear drops. When she came home for a weekend Robert took her to see a doctor as Hanna complained of ear ache. The doctor said that she has a severe ear infection and ear drops should be avoided. He prescribed antibiotics and pain medications to clear up the infection. When Robert returned Hanna to the children's home he informed them of what the doctor said and gave Hanna's medications to them.

The nurse kept placing eardrops in Hanna's ear and that caused her ear drum to burst.

The outcome of that burst eardrum was devastating to Hanna's academic performance in school as she had a hearing problem and had to switch schools. This incident can be seen as medical neglect from the caregivers of Hanna, as stated by the children's act 38 of 2005.

"   8

---

7.   **https://kidshealth.org/en/parents/ptsd.html**

8.   https://www.legalwise.co.za/

Children's rights

May 22, 2023

Facebook[9]Twitter[10]WhatsApp[11]LinkedIn[12]Share[13]

Children's rights

Child neglect in South Africa is on the rise.

As children have experienced neglect at alarming rates in South Africa, it is important to note that the Constitution provides that every child has a fundamental right to the following, amongst other things:

---

9.   https://www.legalwise.co.za/#facebook

10.   https://www.legalwise.co.za/#twitter

11.   https://www.legalwise.co.za/#whatsapp

12.   https://www.legalwise.co.za/#linkedin

13.   https://www.addtoany.com/
share#url_43ec3e5dee6e706af7766fffea512721_https_0bcef9c45bd8a48eda1b26eb0c61c869_
3A_0bcef9c45bd8a48eda1b26eb0c61c869_2F_0bcef9c45bd8a48eda1b26eb0c61c869_2Fwww
.legalwise.co.za_0bcef9c45bd8a48eda1b26eb0c61c869_2Fnews_0bcef9c45bd8a48eda1b26eb0
c61c869_2Fchildrens-rights_6cff047854f19ac2aa52aac51bf3af4a_title_43ec3e5dee6e706af776
6fffea512721_Children_0bcef9c45bd8a48eda1b26eb0c61c869_27s_0bcef9c45bd8a48eda1b2
6eb0c61c869_20rights

> access to basic nutrition, shelter and health care services;

> access to family care and parental care; and

> to be protected from maltreatment, neglect, abuse and degradation.

Child Protection Week runs from 29 May 2023 to 5 June 2023 aiming to bring awareness to children's rights and how they can be protected. In the official statement, it is specifically mentioned that "It is in our hands to stop the cycle of neglect, abuse, violence and exploitation of children." Although abuse and violence are terms that everyone is quite familiar with, neglect is not always something everyone is aware of. This article will focus on what child neglect is and where to report it.

What is child neglect?

> In order to protect a child's best interests and rights, parents and caregivers must be able to provide for the child financially, physically and psychologically (emotional development). This includes the parental rights set out in section 18 of the Children's Act 38 of 2005 ("Children's Act") that provides that parents have the duty to care for the child, maintain contact with the child, act as guardian of the child, and contribute to the maintenance of the child.

> Child neglect can be defined as the failure of a parent or caregiver to sufficiently provide for a child's well-being and healthy development. This includes a failure to provide for a child's physical, intellectual, emotional or social needs, for example:

- failure to provide a child with health care services, basic education, and a safe and stable environment;

- not providing the child with adequate nutrition;

- having very little, to no contact and interaction with the child;

- not allowing children to play and engage with their family or other children; and

- subjecting the child to dangerous and inhumane practices."

Hanna always asked when can she come home to stay with her parents and siblings, but every plea fell on death ears. No voice of the child was ever appointed for Hanna. The story of Hanna didn't end here and the rest of her story will be included into the siblings story further on in the book. Already there is a lot of inconsistencies in Hanna's story and a lot of wrong doings with misconduct and maltreatment.

The following is documentation with names covered for the protection of identity that shows the wrong in this matter.

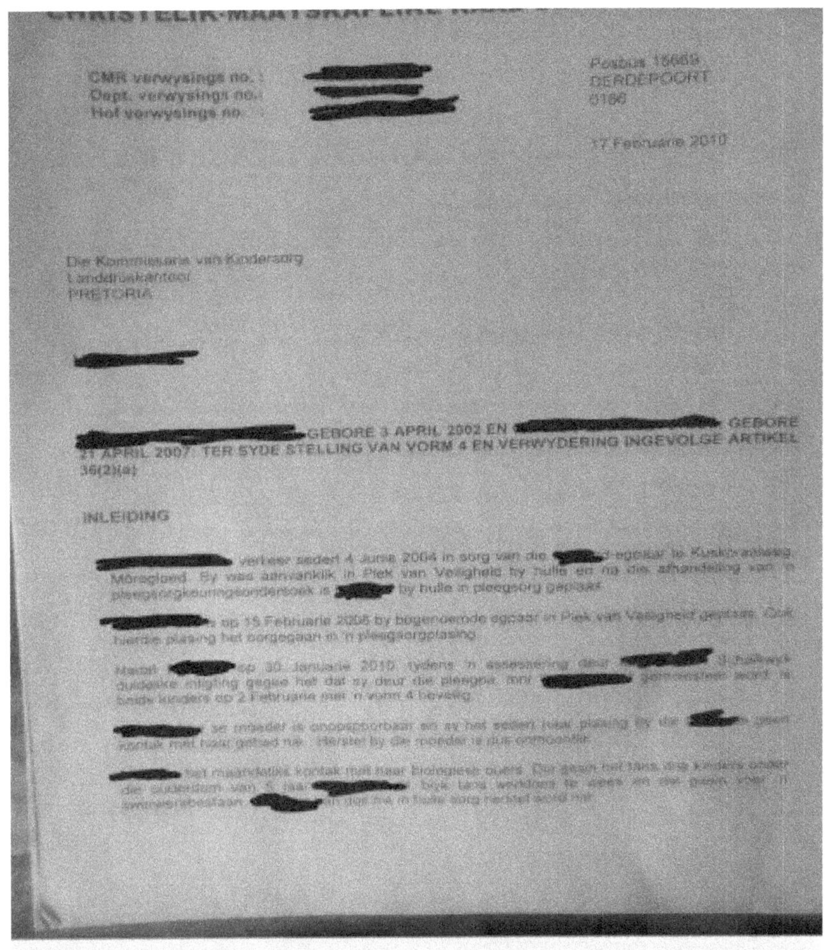

I can not include the psychological report as it is very explicit and detailed in the molestation of Hanna.

The Foster care parents who was now accused of molesting Hanna went to see a attorney because they reckoned that the social workers removed Hanna from their care without sufficient evidence. The went even further to state that removing Hanna from their care was not in her best interest. However the psychological report is very explicit on what has been done to Hanna by MR Niewoudt. A eight year old girl will not have so much detail of sexual behaviour and intercourse if she didn't see it happen or have been exploited her self. Mr and MRS Niewoudt got this Attorneys to fight social services because they removed Hanna from their care. Social services reply was that because they were just Foster parents they had no claim to Hanna. However what fascinates me is the fact that the person who conducted the assessment on Hanna was also called on another document the social workers manager. This brings questions to mind.

There was a AD Hoc meeting for the social services social workers on Hannas case where five people of the same institution had a discussion. On the nodules it states that Hanna was removed from the Niewouds because of molestation and that the Niewouds contacted a attorney and that they will have a meeting with the attorney and the Niewouds where the psychologist will tell them when she would report the matter to the police. Yet no case was ever opened from the psychologist or the social workers.

The following document is of Hanna being placed in the care of the Niewouds where it clearly states they will receive a monthly for the care of Hanna.

There is laws against unfair discrimination in South Africa, but in the case of Hanna the following statements was made to court within reports.

1. Robert is much older than Margaret
2. They live in a house that needs attention

3. Margaret came from a unstable family
4. Mr Roberts arm was amputated
5.

None of these statements placed Hanna in any danger and therefore it was not supposed to be relevant to the matter for her removal.

https://www.justice.gov.za/constitution/chp02.html

In a article written thru Stanford University in 2018 the founding's of the psychological effects of removing a child at a young age from their parents was astonishing.

"Separation from parents removes children's most important protection and generates a new trauma, Stanford scholar says

Stanford psychologist Ian H. Gotlib discusses the psychological effects of early-life stress and parental separation.

In recent months, more than 2,000 migrant children have been separated from their families at the United States/Mexico border. Questions about the policy, including how it affects the children's well-being, has led to a suspension of the practice.

For these children, family separation is an additional trauma to an already adverse experience in their home environments and a long, difficult journey to the United States, according to Stanford psychology Professor Ian H. Gotlib. Even after families are reunited, the uncertainty surrounding these parents' lives could exacerbate feelings of anguish, despair, guilt, blame and depression – negative emotions that disrupt how they learn life skills.

Gotlib's research shows that early life stress is a significant risk factor for depression and suicidal behaviour's. His work has also examined how early life stress affects brain development. His research has also looked at treatments of depression and how to reduce young children's risk of developing depression.

Gotlib is the David Starr Jordan Professor in the Department of Psychology in the Stanford School of Humanities and Sciences. He is a member of Stanford Bio-X, the Child Health Research Institute and the Stanford Neurosciences Institute. He is also the director of the Stanford Neurodevelopment, Affect and Psychopathology Laboratory.

Stanford News Service talked with Gotlib about the impact of early life stress on children's psychological well-being.

One of your research projects examines early life stress. What are the psychological effects of separating children from their parents?

While we do not explicitly study the effects of separating children from their parents in our laboratory, we nevertheless know from decades of research that children, and younger children in particular, depend on and need their parents for their own emotional well-being.

Separation from parents removes children's most important protection and generates a new trauma, Stanford scholar says

Stanford psychologist Ian H. Gotlib discusses the psychological effects of early-life stress and parental separation.

In recent months, more than 2,000 migrant children have been separated from their families at the United States/Mexico border. Questions about the policy, including how it affects the children's well-being, has led to a suspension of the practice.

Ian Gotlib(Image credit: L.A. Cicero)

For these children, family separation is an additional trauma to an already adverse experience in their home environments and a long, difficult journey to the United States, according to Stanford psychology Professor **Ian H. Gotlib**[14]. Even after families are reunited,

---

14.   https://profiles.stanford.edu/ian-gotlib?tab=bio

the uncertainty surrounding these parents' lives could exacerbate feelings of anguish, despair, guilt, blame and depression – negative emotions that disrupt how they learn life skills.

Gotlib's research shows that early life stress is a significant risk factor for depression and suicidal behaviour's. His work **has also examined how early life stress**[15] affects brain development. His research has also looked at treatments of depression and how to reduce young children's risk of developing depression.

Gotlib is the David Starr Jordan Professor in the Department of Psychology in the Stanford School of Humanities and Sciences. He is a member of **Stanford Bio-X**[16], the **Child Health Research Institute**[17] and the **Stanford Neurosciences Institute**[18]. He is also the director of the **Stanford Neurodevelopment, Affect and Psychopathology Laboratory**[19].

Stanford News Service talked with Gotlib about the impact of early life stress on children's psychological well-being.

One of your research projects examines early life stress. What are the psychological effects of separating children from their parents?

While we do not explicitly study the effects of separating children from their parents in our laboratory, we nevertheless know from decades of research that children, and younger children in particular, depend on and need their parents for their own emotional well-being.

<u>Social Sciences</u>[20]

5 questions: How border separations can traumatize

---

15.   http://web.stanford.edu/group/mood/cgi-bin/wordpress/?p=1891

16.   https://biox.stanford.edu/

17.   http://med.stanford.edu/chri.html

18.   https://neuroscience.stanford.edu/

19.   https://web.stanford.edu/group/mood/cgi-bin/wordpress/

20.   https://news.stanford.edu/section/social-sciences/

children[21]

Unplanned separation from parents is among the most damaging events a young child can experience, according to trauma research. A Stanford expert explains how it can hurt kids' development.

In providing a supportive and nurturing relationship, parents play a critical role in promoting their children's healthy development. They also protect their children from the psychological consequences of significant stress by buffering them from the effects of traumas and helping them to regulate their emotions.

Obviously, separation from parents is traumatic; it both removes children's most important protection and generates a new trauma. Indeed, in studies of institutionalized children, such separation has been found to disrupt normal child development and to have long-term negative consequences for their psychological and physical health. In our own research, we are documenting that early adverse experiences have detrimental behavioral and biological consequences for children and adolescents years later.

How does early-life stress affect psychological well-being, both in the short and long term?

Early life stress is consistently associated with behavioral problems in children, with symptoms of psychopathology, and with psychological and physical disorders. It is clear that early life stress can have both immediate and long-lasting consequences, particularly when it is severe and cumulative, as in the case of separation from parents following what might be years of adverse experiences in their home environments and a long, arduous journey to the United States.

We and others have demonstrated that in response to traumas and adverse experiences similar to separation from parents, children secrete high levels of the stress hormone cortisol. This elevated cortisol has negative effects on brain structure and connectivity, slowing neuronal

---

21. http://med.stanford.edu/news/all-news/2018/06/5-questions-how-border-separations-can-traumatize-children.html

growth and reducing volumes of critical brain structures like the hippocampus and affecting brain regions involved in effective emotion regulation. Not surprisingly, research has also demonstrated adverse effects of early trauma on children's psychological functioning, including higher rates of depression, anxiety and "externalizing," or acting-out, behaviour's.

Family separation is one of many stressful experiences of a migrant experience. What can be done to mitigate the effects of stress in childhood?

Obviously, reuniting the migrant children with their parents is an essential first step for mitigating the effects of the stress they have experienced. Certainly, their struggle will not be over, but they are far more likely to then have dedicated and attentive parents who provide nurturance and safety. Research with previously institutionalized children indicates that children can recover from the adverse effects of trauma when they return to family settings.

What psychological effects does family separation have on parents?

Having your child forcibly separated from parents can induce anguish, despair, guilt, blame and depression in the parents – all powerful negative emotions that disrupt how they can learn life skills. This includes how to cope well with adversity, being resilient, not experiencing depression or anxiety.

Unquestionably, for parents, there are few events as traumatic as being separated from their children. Moreover, these emotions are only likely to be exacerbated by the uncertainty surrounding these parents' lives, even after they are reunited with their children.

In our research we have documented powerful negative consequences for children of being raised by parents who are experiencing these negative emotions deeply and for a prolonged period of time. Such children themselves have higher rates of depression and other forms of maladaptive behavior, and have difficulty recovering from stressors and regulating their emotions appropriately. This is a vicious cycle that we must try to end."

https://news.stanford.edu/stories/2018/06/psychological-impact-early-life-stress-parental-separation#:~:text=Not%20surprisingly%2C%20research%20has%20also,exp

We can then for certainty say that removing Hanna from her parents without just cause in the manner it was done caused severe trauma to her at 18 months old. This had a direct impact on Hanna's behaviour later in her life where reports show aggressive tendencies and taking the motherly role in situations. The reports also show that Hanna has trust issues.

Chapter 3: Removal of Hanna's siblings

As previously mentioned Hanna had four other siblings that was born between Margaret and Robert while she was already placed within the system. Jake, Darren, Shane and Olivia.

During 2013 Jake showed inappropriate sexual behaviour towards his brother Darren, Robert saw the problem and went to see a social worker to assist with the behaviour and to find out why Jake acted the way he did. The social worker arranged for a psychological assessment where it was found that Jake was molested by his older nephew. The social worker with Robert opened a case against the nephew. Jake then told the police that the nephew also molested Darren, but after investigation it was found not to be true.

Social services then once again started to intervene with the family circumstances, and made recommendations that was not necessary at all. As set out beneath.

1. All children must attend the social services crèche.
2. Every child must have his or her own room

That was just the beginning of serious problems.

Robert and Margaret was told by social services if they don't enroll their kids in this particular crèche, they will remove the children from their care.

The law states as follow:

As stipulated in the South African Schools Act of 1996, all children between the ages of 7 and 15 are compelled to attend school.

And once again the living circumstances was bought in the reports. Every child needs his own room? No middle class family can afford a six bedroom house, does this mean their children needs to be taken from them?

Jake was in primary school doing grade one and Robert and Margaret enrolled the other three children in social services crèche to avoid them being removed from their care. However with Robert suffering from high blood pressure and heart problems it was difficult to get all the children to school everyday on time. Robert did not have a vehicle at that time and had to walk the about two kilometers with three very small children to school every day while also having to make sure that Jake got on the school bus in time.

Margaret was not of much help with the children so Robert took it upon himself to get every child ready and take them to school by himself. Social services always complained when the children was maybe ten minutes late. Olivia started wetting her bed and pants and she was already fully potty trained. One day Olivia came from the crèche with a red round mark on her leg where she was hit with a jelly baby shoe. Robert reported the incident to the social worker. Shane was tied up with a skipping rope to a chair at this same crèche and their excuse was that he was naughty and it was only for a few minutes. Drake was locked in the bathroom and when he started breaking things the teacher strained him down and he head budded her in the face. All this was reported to the social worker who did nothing to intervene.

Robert then told the social worker he is going to remove his children from the crèche because they are being abused. The social workers reply is nothing more than shocking. "Remove your children from my crèche and I will show you I will remove them from your care."

Any form of physical discipline in South Africa is illegal and should be reported to authorities, yet in this case the social worker threatened the biological parent because he wanted to protect his children from abuse within the crèche. This can also be seen as a blackmailing tactic.

Robert decided he can not let his children go to the crèche anymore and by law they don't need to be in school yet as they all were under seven years old, so he took them out of the crèche.

The social workers then conducted a home visit where they decided that the house needs renovating. They did not take any pictures before they started throwing everything out of the cupboards and made a mess of everything. After the mess was created they took "before" photos but they never took after photos.

One day a social worker showed up at Roberts home after he took the children out of the crèche, with a letter to tell him and Margaret They should attend a round table meeting at the Magistrates Court.

When Robert and Margaret arrived at court it was a full on in camera court proceeding and not a round table meeting as indicated by the social worker. In that court case the "before" photos was submitted to the court with claims that the house is filthy. Robert made a cd with different dates and times with pictures to prove that the house was clean but the Magistrate dismissed that evidence.

In that court proceedings the Magistrate gave a court order for the children to be removed from the family home. But he gave Robert a week with his children to prepare them to go to different places of safety and the Robert should take his children to social services offices. Social services wanted to split the children into different places in different locations. At this point they did not only want to separate the children from the parents but also from each other. A form 36 section 151/152 was used to obtain this court order in 2014. However the form 36 section 151/152 was declared unconstitutional in 2012 by Magistrate Fabricious in the High Court where a full panel of Judges agreed. This fact made the removal unconstitutional but yet the Magistrates court did not question this documentation.

At this point Robert had no knowledge of this illegal document and he never received any form of documentation as he was supposed to receive the court order and the removal form. Social services refused that documentation.

Robert and Margaret went home with their children, they knew that Hanna would also visit that weekend. Robert decided he can not let his children be taken by social services due to having knowledge of what happened with Hanna over the years and the difficulty to have her re unified with them.

So Robert decided to sell all his belongings and his vehicle for a few rands so he can run against the court order with his children. He sold everything during that week and waited for Hanna to come home for the weekend. When Hanna was home he took all five his children and Margaret and fled.

Robert went from one location to the other to keep his children safe. He landed in a place thats like a shelter. There was sufficient food, clothing, housing, running water, electricity and schools provided for them. They were closely supervised by the owner of this shelter no funny business was allowed. The children was safe and well cared for and Robert actually found work as security guard to help with extra things they might need.

Eight months after Robert ran against the court order, after working night shift and resting, social services pitched up at the shelter with the police. Margaret wanted to drink two pain tablets and the officers proceeded to man handle her, she then hit the one police official so they cuffed her in front of the children. Robert and Margaret was placed in the police vehicle while all the children was placed in social services vehicle. While driving to court the social workers interrogated the children about where they were and what they did. Arriving at court the Magistrate was ready and made a new order placing the children together in one place of safety for a period of ninety days for investigation. Hanna and Jake was given the opportunity in court to express what they wanted as they were old enough. Hanna said she wanted to stay with her parents. Jake grabbed at his heart and could hardly breath kept saying my heart, my heart is sore. The Magistrate did not take this into consideration and all children was immediately taken to the Place of Safety.

Soon after Margaret left Robert for good and she did not attempt to make any contact with her children. Margaret never called Robert to ask how the kids was doing. It's as if the children never had a mother. Robert kept fighting to get his children back in his care. But the more he fought the more Social Services estranged him from his children. Visitations was supposed to be once a month for two hours under supervision at the Place of safety, however at some point social services did not schedule this appointments for eight months. Robert emailed the social worker, he send numerous messages and what's app messages and she never responded.

Then one day Robert received a message from Margaret's so called sister as he later found out it was Margaret who send the message, it stated that Margaret is dead. The same message was sent to the Place of Safety. Not the social worker or the Place of Safety investigated or asked Robert if this was true before telling the children their mother passed away. In that message was a date and time for her funeral as well as the church where the service would be conducted. Social services took the children to their mothers so called funeral that did not exist. They then received another message with another date and time as apparently the burial was postponed and once again they took the children without asking Robert, who at this point knew its a lie.

The children wrote letters to their "deceased" mother telling her how they loved her and how much they will miss her. When Robert could see them again they gave that letters to him for safe keeping.

This is the worst form of psychological abuse I have ever heard off and it breaks my heart to think a mother could do this to her children. But I also feel disgust in the social services for not investigating this before disclosing to the children. I can only imagine the pain and the trauma that these kids endured because of this act of cruelty.

After numerous estrangements from his children Robert also endured severe trauma. Everytime when he didn't see his children for long periods because of social workers lack of compliance and he could see them again he was nervous. The reason for this was because everything he would talk about with the children under supervision was mentally recorded by a woman sitting close by, but she then twisted what he said to make him look bad. On some visits the children would tell him that the owner of the place of safety told them he doesn't want them anymore that's why he didn't visit them. Or he had another woman with children he cared for more than them. She told the children that Robert and Margaret was bad parents and they didn't love them. Whenever the children cried about their parents they were beaten or punished. After a few years some of the children started calling her mom. The most bizarre thing was when Shane said that the owner of the place of safety said that they wore refuge bags for nappies because Robert and Margaret could not afford nappies.

Already at this point we can see numerous psychological abuse taking place.

1. Removal from parental home
2. Parental alienation
3. Telling kids parents don't care or live them
4. Not investigating mothers death and taking kids to fake funerals.

Robert attended a panel meeting at the place of safety where the owner and the social worker was present. During this meeting the social worker praised the owner of the place of safety as being a good mother to the children and that she loves his children.

They told Robert that all his children has learning disabilities and that they are receiving extra classes and therapy. Take into account at the time of the panel meeting the children was already three years in the care of this place of safety, with Robert only seeing his children on and off once a month for two hours under supervision. When the children was placed in the place of safety their ages was Hanna 13, Jake 8, Darren 5, Shane 4 and Olivia 3. But yet the owner off the place of safety said "Darren swears at me severely, and it's because he learned it from you Robert." Within this same meeting Robert learned that Darren and Olivia wets their beds every night. At this point Darren was eight and Olivia six.

Looking into data and scientific evidence it is clear that trauma and stressors can cause bed wetting especially if the child was fully potty trained and all of a sudden starts bed wetting again.

https://www.ncbi.nlm.nih.gov/pmc/articles/PMC5020142/

But never did social services or the place of safety investigate the reasons behind the bed wetting.

It later came into the light that the place of safety would punish the children for bed wetting by taking their pocket money to pay someone to wash the bedding or the children had to wash it themselves. A few beatings was also done because of the bed wetting.

"What types of abuse must be reported?

⬦ Any type of abuse must be reported. There are different types of abuse a child may suffer, for example, if a child is:

o injured through physical abuse, for example, being hit or punched by someone that leads to a black eye or bruised lip;

o neglected, for example, physical neglect (such as where a child does not receive food or water) or medical neglect (such as not taking a child to a doctor when s/he child is very sick);

o sexually abused, for example, where a person has sexual relations with a child, such as rape or any other sexual violation; and/or o verbally and emotionally abused, for example, where a child is constantly being humiliated or being threatened with violence."

Some of the most precious times in a child's life is the occasions they look forward to.

Opening presents on Christmas morning

Spending time with friends and family

Going on holiday

Birthday cake

For Darren unfortunately those were times he was rather punished for being a "naughty" boy. One year just before Christmas Robert had a visitation with the children, Darren then nine years old told him that the Place of Safety is taking all the children to the seaside on Christmas morning for a holiday, but the aunty said he will not go because he is naughty. Robert thought maybe she only said that to get Darren to listen. Unfortunately she didn't just say that. After the holidays when Robert went to see his children all the other kids was going on about the lovely time they spend at the ocean, picking up shells etc. Darren just sat there with tears welling up under his eyes. He told Robert on Christmas morning they left him there with a older woman and went to the seaside for a week.

Imagine being a nine year old boy that was removed from his parents and the only thing you have to hold on to is your siblings, but now on a special day like Christmas even your siblings gets taken away and you, you are alone in a place you don't want to be with a older lady. No friends, no family, no singing carols, no presents or sweets like other children. Just you captivated by your own thoughts with the sound of the aunties voice "you are naughty" playing over and over in your head.

On one visitation the children was called inside to take medications, Robert dis not know why his children needed medication or what type of medication were they administered. And the children was to young to tell him, the only thing they could tell him was that they were given this medications daily. When Robert asked the social worker about it she said its classified information and she won't discuss it with him.

At the age of seventeen Hanna ran away from the place of safety. She came to Robert. Even though Robert knew he could get in trouble with the law if he does not call the social worker he told Hanna to stay with him he will protect her. Not the social worker or the Place of Safety called Robert to tell him that Hanna was missing neither did they report her missing at the police station. They did not even search for her. On the second day after Hanna came to Robert she started talking about what happens in the place of safety. "Daddy I ran away because I couldn't take the abuse on my siblings anymore, I needed to get out to safe them from that place." Hanna told Robert about beatings where Darren was the one being severely physically abused, she told Robert about Jake that is called snake and made to wash pig pans and dustbins, Olivia was thrown in the face with a scissor by the owner of the place of safety and Hanna had to help the younger children to bath and was forced to go and work at the owners sons venue for weddings over weekends. The other kids had to go work on the farm during some weekends and holidays. And if Hanna refused she was shouted at and told she is lazy.

Robert took Hanna to the police station to open a case of abuse, child labour. The police officer on duty refused to open a docket stating she must give a avidavid and then Robert must call the social worker and hand it to her to investigate. Robert assisted Hanna with the avidavid and three days later called the social worker. Instead of taking responsibility for not acting on Hanna's disappearance the social worker started the blame game trying to push the whole situation on Robert.

Robert told her about the avidavid and that Hanna is with him. The social worker made a appointment to go and see Robert wich she did. Robert gave her Hanna's avidavid that stated the abuse. The social worker then proceeded to tell Robert they won't bother with Hanna anymore because she is almost eighteen. This avidavid was taken to the perpetrator by the social worker and the case was never investigated properly. Hanna was finally after sixteen years in the welfare system free to do what she wanted to do.

This is what should have been done by the social worker or the place of safety the moment they realised Hanna was gone:

⬦ **Give a good description of what the child was wearing, their last whereabouts and any information that may help the police.**

⬦ **Complete a SAPS 55 (A) form which safeguards the police against false or hoax reports. This form also gives the Police permission to distribute the photos and information of the missing child.**

⬦ **Make sure the police give you a reference number and a contact name and number of the SAPS officer(s) assigned to the investigation.**

Robert asked the social worker that he wanted his other children moved from that place of safety because of the abuse and maltreatment and what surprised him was the speed reply and that they actually for once listened to him.

The matter went back to the Magistrates court where a order was given to move the children to a children's home near Roberts home. The Magistrate also asked why haven't the children been home for weekend visits or holidays in five years and she instructed the social worker to work towards re unification.

At the children's home visitations for Robert was more frequent and went much more smoothly all the supervision was taken away and he could visit his children every weekend Saturday and Sunday. Then on one visit he was told by the children that Olivia and Darren was taken to the police station because Darren had sexual intercourse with Olivia. That didn't make sense to Robert because boys and girls didn't stay in the same homes and Darren was only eleven years old at that time. So Robert called the social worker on the Monday to ask about what the children said. The social worker told Robert that it's a sensitive case and she can't discuss it with him all that she can say is yes there was such incident.

Robert didn't hear anything about this story again and assumed it went dead. The December Robert called the social worker to ask that the children visit him for the holidays, she then told him there is no way as Darren must be in court just before Christmas for charges of rape on his sister Olivia. The matter went to court and Darren who just turned twelve was send to a Secure Care Centre (Juvenile) trail awaiting. The Magistrate on the case wanted criminal capacity to be done. During the time of the alleged incident Darren was 11 years old and Olivia nine. The Criminal Justice Act for minors states as follow:

The CJA is specifically intended for children between the ages 12 and 18. The CJA states that: A child under the age of 12 years cannot be arrested! This means that a child under 12 years does not have criminal capacity and cannot be charged or arrested for an offence.

Yet the Magistrate kept pushing for criminal capacity to be done. This trail went on for ten months with no resolve due to the criminal capacity not being done. The matter was send to Department Public Prosecution and they dismissed the charges against Darren due to a lack of evidence and the age of Darren. Darren spend ten months trail awaiting due to this error by a Magistrate.

Darren was then referred back to children's court for placement in a facility, the children's home refused to take him back and labelled him as a problem child who raped is sister. So the Magistrate send him back to the secure care centre but on the side for children with behavioural problems.

Robert could see that Darren was emotionally not doing good in the Secure centre and asked the social worker to re unify Darren with him. The social worker refused re unification but agreed on a leave of absence for Darren to come home for a month. During that month Darren adapted well with his home environment, started learning to read and acted as a normal boy his age would do although he didn't always listen when talked to I guess that's a normal child's thing. Darren also told Robert during this visit that he was raped three times in one night by other boys in the secure centre. Robert took him to the children's unit to report the matter and Darren was taken to a doctor to examine him with a J88 form that needed to be filled in.

Imagine taking your twelve year old child for a very invasive examination and seeing him blush because he is so self conscious but to make things worse a parents worst nightmare is to hear they want to test your child for HIV. That thought never crossed Roberts mind until the doctor told him it needs to be done. To sit there and wait for the results is nothing but torture. Luckily the test came back negative. The physical examination could not provide evidence of the rape occurring as the doctor said the time frame is to long. The doctor however made a mental state evaluation and said that the incident might have occurred. The case was closed due to insufficient evidence.

Robert made one mistake his nephew with his wife and two kids was homeless, it was cold and raining and they were stuck in a car under a bridge. Robert told them come stay here in the outside room until you guys get back on your feet. Robert by this time also had a new woman in his life who had a daughter of four years old at that time. All the children was told to play where they can be seen by adults at all times. But one afternoon Darren was sitting at he back of the yard the adults could see him but the little girl and one of the other boys was nowhere to be seen. The little girls mother called her and she came out behind a wooden cabin with that boy age nine behind her.

Later that evening when the girls mother took her to Bath the girl told her that the boy of nine wanted her to pull down her pants and underwear. As a mother would do the mother went straight to Roberts nephew and told him to tell his boy that it is wrong to tell small girls to take down their pants. The mother of the boy however blew it totally out of per portion and knowing the claims against Darren she went straight to the social worker and laid off a false statement. She said that Darren threatened her boy to tell the girl to pull down her pants and that Darren wanted her son to have sexual intercourse with the little girl. A case once again was opened against Darren for inappropriate sexual misconduct and instigating rape.

However at this point neither Robert or his finance knew about these statements or case that has been made. Robert had to be back in court with Darren that day would have been a permanent re unification. On arrival at court the attorney asked Roberts fiancé to speak in private, where he told her about the case opened and the statement and that they won't place Darren back in his father's care that day. Robert was furious as he knew Darren was not guilty of anything but yet the social worker, the court is condemning him once again. Darren was then send back to the secure care centre trail awaiting. The manner in wich the social worker took Darren from Robert was inhumane. She stood laughing with the court clerks while Darren clung to Rina crying " Mommy please don't let them take me away, I don't want to go." The fear of Darren was real. Rinas daughter sat on the steps inside the magistrates court crying, "don't let them take my brother." The social worker grabbed Darren by his arm and started walking, not looking back for one second while Darren cried and Robert stood there angry, hurt, crying. The Department of Social Development social workers as present in court that day, but they couldn't intervene as the case was not fully on their files yet. Later on the social worker of Department of Social Development in a panel meeting broke down and said that was the most horrific, inhumane case she ever saw in a children's court. What stood out from this was that no case number could be provided in court but yet the Magistrate gave the order on the hearsay of the social worker. No proper investigation was done yet, but the child is placed in trail awaiting.

Roberts fiancé took her little girl to the investigating officer so the children's unit could take a statement from her about what happened. Within that statement the girl described the days events her words "Darren didn't play with us, he was sitting in the back of the yard, that boy called me behind the cabin and told me I must pull down my pants." The little girls statement cleared Darren's case. Although he was then send straight back to behavioural problems.

In the meantime in the children's home where the other children was Jake got beaten up severely with a broken nose. Olivia spoke about the house mother showing her a movie on her phone about a woman cutting open another woman's tummy and drinking the blood, she spoke about frogs coming out of people. Olivia told Robert the older girls takes her dolls and throws them away. Olivia dressed provokingly and seemed overall under the influence of some medication. Shane was pulled back, bleak with dark circles under his eyes he told Robert about constant fights he was involved in. Shane told Robert that when he is naughty he gets either dry bread and water or pap with salt and vinegar to eat. He was locked in his room on numerous occasions. The house father threw him against a wall and the relieve house mother strangled him. This was all very disturbing to Robert so he wanted to report this matters to the social worker, but to his surprise was told oh you guys don't have a outside social worker anymore. So no weekend visits or holidays could be arranged because there is no social worker.

Roberts fiancé, Rina then decided no more, she could see the devastation and the hurt that Robert was enduring so she started studying the children's act 38 of 2005 in conjunction with the Constitutional laws. During this time she started looking into court orders and registrations. And this is where she found out that a form

36 removal was unconstitutional by using section 151/152. And this is exactly the forms that was used to remove all Roberts children from his care in the first place.

https://www.saflii.org/za/cases/ZACC/2012/1.html

1

C and Others v Department of Health and Social Development, Gauteng and Others (CCT 55/11) [2012] ZACC 1; 2012 (2) SA 208 (CC); 2012 (4) BCLR 329 (CC) (11 January 2012)

Download original files Links to summary

PDF format[2]   PDF format[4]

RTF format[3]   RTF format[5]

CONSTITUTIONAL COURT OF SOUTH AFRICA

---

1.   https://www.saflii.org/

2. https://www.saflii.org/za/cases/ZACC/2012/1.pdf

3. https://www.saflii.org/za/cases/ZACC/2012/1.rtf

4. https://www.saflii.org/za/cases/ZACC/2012/1media.pdf

5. https://www.saflii.org/za/cases/ZACC/2012/1media.doc

Case CCT 55/11

[2012] ZACC 1[6]

In the matter between:

C ....First Applicant

M ....Second Applicant

CENTRE FOR CHILD LAW ....Third Applicant

and

DEPARTMENT OF HEALTH AND SOCIAL DEVELOPMENT, GAUTENG ....First Respondent

CITY OF TSHWANE METROPOLITAN MUNICIPALITY ....Second Respondent

ITERELENG RESIDENTIAL FACILITY FOR THE DISABLED ....Third Respondent

DESMOND TUTU PLACE OF SAFETY ....Fourth Respondent

PABALELO PLACE OF SAFETY ....Fifth Respondent

MINISTER FOR POLICE ....Sixth Respondent

MINISTER FOR SOCIAL DEVELOPMENT ....Seventh Respondent

---

6.   https://www.saflii.org/cgi-bin/LawCite?cit=%5b2012%5d%20ZACC%201

Heard on : 16 August 2011
   Decided on : 11 January 2012

JUDGMENT

SKWEYIYA J (Froneman J concurring):

Introduction

1. This case concerns the confirmation of a declaration of constitutional invalidity of sections 151 and 152 of the Children's Act.[1] The North Gauteng High Court, Pretoria (High Court) declared these sections unconstitutional to the extent that they provide for a child to be removed from family care by state officials and placed in temporary safe care, but do not provide for the child to be brought before the children's court for automatic review of that removal.[2] In terms of section 172(2)(a) of the Constitution, an order of constitutional invalidity by a High Court must be referred to this Court for confirmation, without which it will have no force.[3] More precisely, therefore, this case concerns the constitutionality of the statutory framework for the removal of children from their family environment and their placement in temporary safe care at the instance of the state.

Statutory framework

2. It is necessary first to set out the current statutory framework for the removal of children from family care by state officials. Chapter 9 of the Children's Act regulates the treatment of children deemed to be in need of care and protection.[4] This Chapter contemplates two routes for the removal of these children to temporary safe care: section

---

1. https://www.saflii.org/za/cases/ZACC/2012/1.html#sdfootnote1sym

2. https://www.saflii.org/za/cases/ZACC/2012/1.html#sdfootnote2sym

3. https://www.saflii.org/za/cases/ZACC/2012/1.html#sdfootnote3sym

4. https://www.saflii.org/za/cases/ZACC/2012/1.html#sdfootnote4sym

151 provides for removal by court order, while section 152 provides for removal without a court order in certain circumstances.

3. Section 151(1) empowers the children's court, if it appears from testimony before it that a child is in need of care and protection, to order that a social worker investigate the matter and report back within 90 days.[5] Section 151(2) further empowers the court, before receiving the report, to order that the child be removed and placed in temporary safe care, if this appears necessary for the safety and well-being of the child.[6] Section 151(3) preserves the court's general powers in respect of investigations.[7] Section 151(4) requires a removal order to identify the child in sufficient detail for the order to be executed.[8] Section 151(5) and (6) affords authorised people and accompanying police officials extensive powers to effect the removal of a child.[9] Section 151(7) requires the person who has removed a child to give notice of that fact to the child's parent, guardian or care-giver and the provincial department of social development.[10] Section 151(8) requires the court to consider all relevant facts, with the best interests of the child being the determining factor in any decision regarding removal.[11]

5. https://www.saflii.org/za/cases/ZACC/2012/1.html#sdfootnote5sym

6. https://www.saflii.org/za/cases/ZACC/2012/1.html#sdfootnote6sym

7. https://www.saflii.org/za/cases/ZACC/2012/1.html#sdfootnote7sym

8. https://www.saflii.org/za/cases/ZACC/2012/1.html#sdfootnote8sym

9. https://www.saflii.org/za/cases/ZACC/2012/1.html#sdfootnote9sym

10. https://www.saflii.org/za/cases/ZACC/2012/1.html#sdfootnote10sym

11. https://www.saflii.org/za/cases/ZACC/2012/1.html#sdfootnote11sym

4. Section 152(1) empowers a social worker or police official to remove a child and place the child in temporary safe care, without a court order, if it is reasonably believed that: (a) the child is in need of care and protection and needs immediate emergency protection; (b) the delay in obtaining a court order may jeopardise the child's safety and well-being; and (c) removal is the best way to secure the child's safety and well-being.[12] Thereafter notice of that removal must be given to the child's parent, guardian or care-giver, the clerk of the children's court and the provincial department of social development.[13] Section 152(4) requires the removing authority to consider all relevant facts, with the best interests of the child being the determining factor.[14] Section 152(5), (6) and (7) imposes serious penalties for misuse of the power to remove a child without a court order,[15] and section 152(8) requires compliance with a prescribed procedure.[16]

5. Section 155(1) requires that the children's court must decide whether a child, who was removed in terms of section 151 or section 152, is in need of care and protection.[17] Section 155(2) provides that a social worker must investigate and compile a report on the matter within 90 days, before the child is brought before the children's court.[18] Section 155(6), (7) and (8) enumerates the orders

---

12. https://www.saflii.org/za/cases/ZACC/2012/1.html#sdfootnote12sym

13. https://www.saflii.org/za/cases/ZACC/2012/1.html#sdfootnote13sym

14. https://www.saflii.org/za/cases/ZACC/2012/1.html#sdfootnote14sym

15. https://www.saflii.org/za/cases/ZACC/2012/1.html#sdfootnote15sym

16. https://www.saflii.org/za/cases/ZACC/2012/1.html#sdfootnote16sym

17. https://www.saflii.org/za/cases/ZACC/2012/1.html#sdfootnote17sym

the children's court may make once the child has been brought before it.[19]

6. In summary, the current statutory framework for the removal of children from their families at the instance of the state contemplates two procedural routes for removal. Firstly, a person may testify to the children's court that a particular child is in need of care and protection, and the court may order the immediate removal of the child if this appears necessary for the child's safety and well-being.[20] Secondly, a designated social worker or police official may remove a child without a court order, if there is reason to believe that this is required urgently.[21] In both cases, a social worker will be required to compile a report on whether the child is in need of care and protection, within 90 days, after which the child must be brought before the children's court for a determination of whether she or he is indeed in need of care and protection.[22] There is no provision for automatic court review before compilation of the report.

Factual background

7. The first and second applicants are, respectively, Mr C, father of a girl aged three, and Ms M, mother of two girls aged one and four. The third applicant is the Centre for Child Law, a law clinic established by the University of

18. https://www.saflii.org/za/cases/ZACC/2012/1.html#sdfootnote18sym

19. https://www.saflii.org/za/cases/ZACC/2012/1.html#sdfootnote19sym

20. https://www.saflii.org/za/cases/ZACC/2012/1.html#sdfootnote20sym

21. https://www.saflii.org/za/cases/ZACC/2012/1.html#sdfootnote21sym

22. https://www.saflii.org/za/cases/ZACC/2012/1.html#sdfootnote22sym

Pretoria, participating in this matter as an institutional applicant, in the public interest and in the interests of children in similar circumstances to the children of Mr C and Ms M.[23]

8. The first respondent is the Department of Health and Social Development, Gauteng (Department). The second respondent is the City of Tshwane Metropolitan Municipality (City). The third, fourth and fifth respondents are, respectively, Itereleng Residential Facility for the Disabled, Desmond Tutu Place of Safety and Pabalelo Place of Safety, which are care facilities under the direction of the Department. They play no part in these proceedings. The sixth respondent is the Minister for Police and the seventh respondent is the Minister for Social Development, who is responsible for the administration of the Children's Act. The first, sixth and seventh respondents have jointly made submissions in these proceedings and are referred to collectively as the state.

9. On Friday 13 August 2010, Mr C was conducting his trade of repairing shoes at a prominent intersection in Pretoria, as he does daily, but he was accompanied on that day by his daughter. His partner, who usually looked after her during the day, was in hospital giving birth. Ms M, who begs for her living, was present at the same intersection that day, accompanied by an assistant, as she is blind, and by her two daughters.

10. Social workers employed by the Department, together with officials from the City, had planned, for that day, an operation involving the removal of children from people

---

23. https://www.saflii.org/za/cases/ZACC/2012/1.html#sdfootnote23sym

found to be begging while accompanied by children. This operation was well-planned and publicised, but no court order had been sought for the removal of these children. In execution of the operation, social workers removed Mr C's and Ms M's children from their care, and placed them in the Department's care facilities, without notifying the parents of where they were.

Proceedings in the High Court

11. Mr C and Ms M, together with the Centre for Child Law, promptly approached the High Court with a two-part application. In Part 1, they applied, on an urgent basis, for an order to restore their children to their care. On 24 August 2010, the High Court (per Preller J) ordered that Mr C's daughter be returned immediately to his care and that Ms M's children remain at the place of safety for five weeks, pending an investigation into whether they needed alternative care.[24] By order of the children's court, they have since been returned to Ms M's care, under the supervision of a social worker.[25]

12. In Part 2, the applicants sought, among other things: (a) a declaratory order in relation to the conduct of the social workers; and (b) a declaration of constitutional invalidity of sections 151 and 152 of the Children's Act, to the extent that they fail to provide for judicial review of removal and placement decisions made by social workers or police. This relief was initially opposed by the state, but subsequently was the subject of agreement between the parties, resulting

---

24. https://www.saflii.org/za/cases/ZACC/2012/1.html#sdfootnote24sym

25. https://www.saflii.org/za/cases/ZACC/2012/1.html#sdfootnote25sym

in a draft order handed up to the High Court on 20 January 2011. Nevertheless, written argument was filed and oral argument was heard on 13 May 2011.

13. On 27 May 2011, the High Court (per Fabricius J) observed that, if a child is removed in terms of section 152 of the Children's Act, the matter will be heard for the first time by the children's court after the 90 days within which the social worker is required to investigate and compile a report.[26] In contrast, its predecessor, section 12 of the repealed Child Care Act,[27] required that a child removed without a warrant had to be brought before a court within 48 hours for a formal determination of whether that removal was justified, which would also allow a parent to appear and to challenge the removal.[28] The High Court found that, although section 152 does require the person conducting a removal to notify the parent, guardian or care-giver of the child, as well as the clerk of the children's court, this does not amount to a notice to appear in court, as was required under the repealed Child Care Act.[29]

14. The High Court held that this clearly does not create an opportunity for automatic review of the removal within a reasonable timeframe, and that the lacuna created by the Children's Act renders the legislation procedurally deficient, with inadequate protective mechanisms in place to ensure that drastic interference with the child's right to parental

---

26. https://www.saflii.org/za/cases/ZACC/2012/1.html#sdfootnote26sym

27. https://www.saflii.org/za/cases/ZACC/2012/1.html#sdfootnote27sym

28. https://www.saflii.org/za/cases/ZACC/2012/1.html#sdfootnote28sym

29. https://www.saflii.org/za/cases/ZACC/2012/1.html#sdfootnote29sym

care is not arbitrary, unreasonable or unjust.[30] The lacuna is compounded by section 155, which strongly implies that there will be no review of the removal until after the receipt of the social worker's report, and that the issue at that stage would not be whether the removal was justified, but rather whether the child is in need of care and protection and, if so, what the best outcome would be.[31] The High Court concluded that the state has a duty to put in place measures that ensure the best interests of the child at all times, and that specific provision for the review of removals is a minimum requirement of that duty.[32]

15. Consequently, the High Court declared sections 151 and 152 of the Children's Act unconstitutional to the extent that they fail to provide for a child, who has been removed in terms of those sections and placed in temporary safe care, to be brought before the children's court for a review of the removal and placement in temporary safe care.[33] The Court further made an interim order, pending confirmation of the order of constitutional invalidity by this Court, to the effect that certain words would be read in to the impugned provisions to remedy the unconstitutionality, as follows:

"18.1. Section 151(7) and Section 152(7) of the Act is to read as though the following appears as Section (d):

'(d) within 48 hours, place the matter before the Children's Court having jurisdiction for a review of the removal and

30. https://www.saflii.org/za/cases/ZACC/2012/1.html#sdfootnote30sym

31. https://www.saflii.org/za/cases/ZACC/2012/1.html#sdfootnote31sym

32. https://www.saflii.org/za/cases/ZACC/2012/1.html#sdfootnote32sym

33. https://www.saflii.org/za/cases/ZACC/2012/1.html#sdfootnote33sym

continued placement of the child, give notice of the date and time of the review to the child's parent, guardian or caregiver, and cause the child to be present at the review proceedings where practicable.'

18.2. Section 152(3)(b) of the Act is to read as if the following words appear therein:

18.2.1. 'without delay but within 24 hours' immediately before the word 'refer'; and

18.2.2. 'to place the matter before the children's court for review as contemplated in section 152(2)(d)' immediately before the words 'for investigation'

18.3. Section 152(3)(b) of the Act will accordingly read as follows:

'(b) without delay but within 24 hours refer the matter to a designated social worker to place the matter before the children's court for review as contemplated in section 152(2)(d) and for investigation contemplated in section 155(2); and'

18.4. Section 155(2)(b) of the Act is to read as if the words 'Before the child is brought before the children's court,' appearing immediately before the words 'a designated social worker' have been deleted there from."

Proceedings in this Court

16. On 20 June 2011, the applicants approached this Court under rule 16(4),[34] seeking an order confirming the High

---

34. https://www.saflii.org/za/cases/ZACC/2012/1.html#sdfootnote34sym

Court's order of constitutional invalidity, but varying it to correct certain typographical errors in the original order. Confirmation is not opposed by any party. An application was made from the bar by the applicants and the state, seeking an amendment of Form 36 of the Regulations to the Children's Act to include a notice to the parents or family of a child, removed in terms of section 151 or 152 of the Children's Act, to appear in the children's court for a review of the removal.

17. The applicants submit that the absence of a provision for automatic review of the removal and placement in temporary safe care of a child is in breach of children's constitutional rights to family care or parental care, the best interests of the child being considered paramount and the rights to dignity and privacy to the extent that they include and protect the right to family life. The balancing of these rights is necessary. But a critical part of this balancing is automatic review of the removal of the child. This requirement, which was provided for in the repealed Child Care Act, is also a cornerstone of international law relating to the removal of children. Its absence from the Children's Act, it is argued, thus represents a retrogressive step.

18. The applicants contend that the inherent right of review of administrative actions, enshrined in section 33 of the Constitution,[35][35] is insufficient to provide adequate protection of the best interests of the child for four reasons: (a) section 155(2) of the Children's Act strongly implies that there will be no review of the removal; (b) even if there is such a right, it would require an application to be brought

---

35. https://www.saflii.org/za/cases/ZACC/2012/1.html#sdfootnote35sym

by the parent or child, which is too onerous a burden; (c) the removal of a child from parental care is a serious infringement of important rights, which gives the state an additional duty to take steps to ensure the best interests of the child, a minimum requirement of which is automatic review; and (d) given the number of people affected by the provision, it must make expressly clear that automatic review is required in all cases. Thus, the order of constitutional invalidity must be confirmed.

19. The applicants urge that, subject to the correction of the error identified in the notice of motion, the order of the High Court is sufficient to cure the constitutional invalidity.[36] Parliament would be entitled to amend the provisions at a later stage should it seek a different solution.

20. The state associates itself with the applicants' submissions. However, in addition to the reasons advanced by the applicants, the state contends that the impugned sections are unconstitutional because they infringe section 34 of the Constitution,[37] in that they oust the jurisdiction of the children's court for a period of 90 days, during which time nobody may access the court. Further, the limitation of constitutional rights is neither reasonable nor justifiable under section 36 of the Constitution.

Condonation

21. The applicants requested condonation for their failure to comply with rule 16(4), as they had not annexed the correct

---

36. https://www.saflii.org/za/cases/ZACC/2012/1.html#sdfootnote36sym

37. https://www.saflii.org/za/cases/ZACC/2012/1.html#sdfootnote37sym

High Court order to their main application papers. I would grant condonation.

Issues for determination

22. The following broad issues arise for determination:
1. Are any rights limited by the impugned provisions?
2. If so, are these limitations reasonable and justifiable?
3. If not, what are the appropriate remedies?

Are any rights limited by the impugned provisions?

23. The coercive removal of a child from her or his home environment is undoubtedly a deeply invasive and disruptive measure. Uninvited intervention by the state into the private sphere of family life threatens to rupture the integrity and continuity of family relations, and even to disgrace the dignity of the family, both parents and children, in their own esteem as well as in the eyes of their community. Both sections 151 and 152 of the Children's Act authorise removals, yet neither section subjects removals to automatic review, which would enable the affected family, including the removed child, to make representations on whether removal was in the best interests of the child. Accordingly, it must be determined whether the impugned provisions impose limitations on any rights enshrined in the Constitution.

24. The removal of a child from the reach of her or his family clearly constitutes a limitation of the child's right to "family care or parental care" in terms of section 28(1)(b) of the Constitution.[38] Although section 28(1)(b) itself also

---

38. https://www.saflii.org/za/cases/ZACC/2012/1.html#sdfootnote38sym

contemplates "appropriate alternative care when removed from the family environment", this is a secondary right, not an equivalent alternative right. It does not necessarily render a removal constitutionally compatible with the primary right to family care or parental care. If that were the case, the primary right would be entirely superfluous and legally meaningless, and section 28(1)(b) would entrench only a right to appropriate care, irrespective of environment. In my view, Van Dijkhorst J was correct in his interpretation of section 28(1)(b) in *Jooste v Botha*,[39] namely that it envisages—

"a child in [the] care of somebody who has custody over him or her. To that situation every child is entitled. That situation the State is constitutionally obliged to establish, safeguard and foster. The State may not interfere with the integrity of the family."[40]

25. This interpretation is fortified by the formulation of the right in international law, which we are bound by section 39(1)(b) of the Constitution to consider.[41] The African Charter on the Rights and Welfare of the Child (ACRWC)[42] provides that "[e]very child shall be entitled to the enjoyment of parental care and protection and shall, whenever possible, have the right to reside with his or her parents",[43] while the United Nations Convention of the

39. https://www.saflii.org/za/cases/ZACC/2012/1.html#sdfootnote39sym

40. https://www.saflii.org/za/cases/ZACC/2012/1.html#sdfootnote40sym

41. https://www.saflii.org/za/cases/ZACC/2012/1.html#sdfootnote41sym

42. https://www.saflii.org/za/cases/ZACC/2012/1.html#sdfootnote42sym

43. https://www.saflii.org/za/cases/ZACC/2012/1.html#sdfootnote43sym

Rights of the Child (UNCRC)[44] guarantees every child's right "to know and be cared for by his or her parents",[45] and "to preserve his or her identity, including . . . family relations as recognized by law without unlawful interference".[46]

26. That section 28 creates distinct rights that are not subject to a single internal qualification is also apparent from this Court's decision in *Fitzpatrick*:[47]

At this point when social services realised that Rina was busy uncovering all the inconsistencies regarding this case, they quickly appointed a new social worker to the case. Rina refused to work with this NPO institution as they deliberately tried in all means to start meddling with her daughter as well. Questions about where her four year old is going to school, wanting a copy of the girls birth certificate made Rina ask questions as the case was not about her or her daughter it was with Robert and his children. Then the social worker wanted Rina to sign a working agreement with the NPO but this working agreement was totally unconstitutional as Rina was not the biological parent to Roberts children yet the social worker wanted Rina to sign documents that gives the NPO full guardianship over Roberts children and should the children be taken to any doctor etc Robert will have no say in any procedure done but the invoice will be send to him. The working agreement also stated that the social worker can at anytime of any day do a home visit and take children where she wanted them without any resilience from Robert. What was even more alarming to Rina was the fact that no names or registrations or intend was filled in

44. https://www.saflii.org/za/cases/ZACC/2012/1.html#sdfootnote44sym

45. https://www.saflii.org/za/cases/ZACC/2012/1.html#sdfootnote45sym

46. https://www.saflii.org/za/cases/ZACC/2012/1.html#sdfootnote46sym

47. https://www.saflii.org/za/cases/ZACC/2012/1.html#sdfootnote47sym

on this document by the social worker, that meant one thing, the social worker can fill in whatever she wanted afterwards. So Rina refused to sign these documents. On a separate occasion the social worker brought two colleagues with to try and intimidate Ria to sign the documents she still refused. Rina had to do police clearance and be checked on the sexual offenders list because she stayed with Robert and the social worker refused starting the re unification if it was not done.

For two years this social worker gave numerous rules and tricks to not start the re unification. That didn't stop Rina she kept learning. Then one day Rina decided its enough and wrote a long letter to all relevant departments and the government pleading for assistance, she included evidence of falsified documents, unconstitutional court orders, abuse. That letter went from the Government to the Provincial Department of Social Development for investigation.

The department of social development started working on the case in a matter of days and Rina was taken to their offices where she spend three hours and then again eight hours to show them the inconsistencies in the matter. They immediately took the case over from the NPO and appointed a social worker from the Department. Rina then found out that Darren is in the Secure Care without a court order. She then contacted the social worker and asked him " against who can I lay charges for kidnapping" as Darren is illegally kept in the Secure Care. That next day Darren was re unified with Robert.

Darren was in a total state of trauma he had severe night terrors, was scared of the dark and other cultural groups. Darren ate excessive to sooth himself. He was always in self protection mode. Darren was re unified with a bag full of antipsychotic medications. When Rina asked why this medications was necessary no one could answer her. On visiting the mental institution to get Darren's medications Rina asked the psychiatrist why Darren needed this medications. Darren was diagnosed with Conduct disorder and ADHD.

Darren had severe intellectual disabilities as well and academically he was severely delayed due to the fact he did not attend any school in three years while in the welfare system.

The same people who remove children from parental care should they neglect to place children in schools was now the same people who disregarded the child's right to a education. The same people who remove children from parental homes if they abuse and neglect their children is now the people who let's children get abused, degraded, humiliated, neglected.

Darren started disclosing what happened in the Secure Care centre. When the children does not obey they get placed in lock down, it's a dark room that's closed. Should they fight the whole community gets called to beat them they also call it Community.

Darren had several tattoos on his body done by "inmates" with melted tires and needles the other children got when taken to court and placed in police cells. That is used needles that's been used for drug addiction in the prison cells. Children gets taken to court in hand cuffs, making them look like hardened criminals. Darren talked a lot about satanic rituals and demons stalking them inside the Secure Care, for months Darren believed that something is in his room out to get him.

No proper trauma counselling was ever provided for Darren and no full psychological assessment was ever done.

Soon after the Department SOCIAL development social took over a court date was set to do the re unification of the other children that was still within the children's home. On the day of the court proceedings Rina was for the first time allowed in court, all previous attempts to attend was denied with the excuse that she is not the biological parent, however she would have to play a crucial role in the care of the children when they were re unified. Also Rina had to do screenings and prove her income as well. And whenever the NPO social worker wanted to know something about the children she would ask Rina. But Rina was disregarded by the children's court.

During this proceeding the Voice of The Child was present, she told the Magistrate that Shane could no longer be in the children's home due to his behaviour that they can't control. Furthermore she said that Jake will soon turn eighteen and then he would have to go but she also stated that there needs to be socio emotional assessment done on the children before releasing them. The voice of the child discredited Department SOCIAL Development by saying they make promises they don't keep. The Magistrate disregarded the social workers report completely and only listened to the voice of the child who by the way was present with the Magistrate before the social worker, Rina and Robert could enter the court. On further investigation it was found that the voice of the child already had the socio emotional assessment of the children she just never submitted it to court. This could be seen as a stalling technique. The Magistrate then proceeded to keep the children in the children's home for another thirty days awaiting the assessments. On Rina's question to the Magistrate on why postponing the inevitable the Magistrate said that Rina would not be allowed to question the courts decision.

The children came home for weekend visits with a leave of absence to start the re unification process but that in it self was traumatic. They would go home on Friday afternoon and on Sunday they would be taken back to the children's home everytime they cried severely when they had to go back.

At the next court date Shane and Jake was re unified with Robert and a order was made for Olivia to stay in the children's home for another two years to receive counselling because of the trauma of being raped while in the children's home.

The boys came home also with bags of anti psychotic medications on high dosages with no background or explanation as to why they are on this medications. Rina received the children's medical cards for visitations to a mental institution where they receive their medications.

The first two weeks of all the boys being home it was peaceful and a lot of laughter and play took place. Then one morning Shane and Darren got into a fight, Shane was excessively angry screaming, swearing and hitting his head against the wall. This outburst lasted for about thirty minutes, while Rina and Robert try to get him to calm down Darren would keep on provoking him causing escalation to the problem.

The next day Jake had the same extreme violent outburst swearing, screaming, hitting using the exact same phrases and words as Shane the previous day just adding one or two extra swear words. Everyday it would be either Jake or Shane having this severe anger outbursts, the boys would hit each other, swear at each other, threaten each other.

Then one day Darren and Jake got into a massive fight where they beat each other with fists Darren picked up a brick and thru Jake on his back with it. There was blood. Jake ran to the streets screaming bloody murder. Rina took all the kids to the mental institution to try and find out what was wrong with them. There the psychiatrist told her that Shane was diagnosed with ADHD and Conduct disorder with markers of Bi Polar, Jake was diagnosed with Bi Polar, Conduct disorder.

Although Rina had diplomas in Mental Health and Psychology she never heard of Conduct Disorder and didn't understand the condition so she went for psych education at the mental institution to try and understand the boys behaviour. All suggestions made to her on handling this outbursts did not work with this boys.

In school Darren and Jake was always in trouble for fighting but especially Darren he was in constant fighting mode. Everything triggered him. Shane was not yet in school as he was awaiting placement from the department of education but also Robert and Rina knew if he was placed in school he would be Expelled within a week due to his very violent behaviour. Each boy had his own challenges and they were busy destructing each other as well as the home and the mental well being of Robert and Rina and her daughter.

Jakes behaviour:
Lying
Manipulating
Stealing
Swearing
Hitting walls and cupboards and his brothers
Refuse to bath
Refuse to make his bed or clean his surroundings
Breaking things in the home
Blame shifting
No respect for adults or people in general
Shane's Behaviour:
Hitting cupboards and brothers
Swearing
Screaming
Excessive stealing
Lying
Manipulating
Hitting head against the wall
Breaking everything glass
Threatening
Running into streets screaming
Refuse to make bed or clean surroundings
Blame shifting
No respect for other children
Darren's Behaviour:
Stabbing with knives, sticks, scissors anything he could get hold
of
Swearing
Hitting
Kicking
Lying

Stealing
Manipulating
Breaking things in and around the home
Blame shifting
No respect for adults or people in general

This behaviour did not get better but rather escalated. The more Rina and Robert tried to get the children to feel safe and loved the more fights came. They didn't want to part take in any family responsibilities. Take into consideration their ages.

Darren 14, Jake 16, Shane 13

Yet everyday it was a struggle to get them to brush teeth, bath, clean their room, make their beds. They only wanted to take part when there was something nice they wanted.

On one occasion Shane totally went off he kept screaming and fighting throwing rocks at his siblings threatening he will kill them hit a hole in the bedroom ceiling. This went on for three hours straight. Rina then took Shane to hospital to be admitted for seventy two hour observation so he can be transferred to the mental institution for evaluation. After the seventy two hour observation Shane was admitted in the mental hospital but because of a Hernia that Shane had for seven years that was not fixed within the welfare system Shane could only stay in the mental institution for a week because his hernia operation was scheduled for the next week.

Shane went for the operation and two days after the operation he once again had a total breakdown. Rina took him back to the mental institution where he was admitted for another three months. During this time Shane was diagnosed with psychosis. He was sent for brain scans and tests and received counselling. After three months he was send home with new medications and he also received injections to try and control his anger a libido injection was also added. For about two weeks Shane was stable then his behaviour escalated once again. He was again admitted to the mental institution for another three months. During this time Rina asked the social worker to do urgent intervention and assist to get Shane in a place where its more structured and where he could be helped extensively. Shane unfortunately had to go to the Secure Care centre that Darren was previously placed in because that was the only place a certain assessment could be done that was needed to get Shane to a place that specialises in children with behaviour problems specifically Conduct Disorder.

In the meantime Jake was also very aggressive and was constantly causing drama, being seventeen at the time the only solution was to get him re evaluated as well. He was taken for the seventy two hour observation that lasted almost a week however the mental institution didn't admit him they just adapted his medications also starting him on anger injections and libido with high doses of mood stabilisers. His moods was very irregular but more controllable at that point. However when he turned eighteen he was an adult by law and he decided that he doesn't need the medications. Jake stopped taking medications, started misusing alcohol and drugs. Robert and Rina sent him to a very good rehab where he could also learn some skills like upholstery, building, welding etc.

But Jake messed up the opportunity by threatening the people with knives, swearing and placing a belt around his neck pretending he would commit suicide. The rehab threw him out stating he needs to get stabilised and take his medications then he can go back. Jake refused any help or intervention Robert and Rina introduced. He ran away from home stayed on the streets and had street gang fights often. People would tell Rina that Jake is dirty and always under the influence of alcohol. Rina once saw Jake eight o clock in the morning coming out of a bottle store with a drink in his hand, he pretended he didn't know her. Jake totally went off the rails and there was nothing more Robert or Rina could do to help him.

Then Darren at that point fifteen years old started self destruction he also wanted to life the life that Jake had. Darren could not understand that Jake is an adult making wrong decisions and he is a minor who needs his father's guidance. So Darren started slipping out of the home early mornings and coming back late evenings grabbing his plate of food eating, leaving his dirty dishes everywhere even in his room just to repeat it the next day. Darren assaulted another learner in school and at that stage was Expelled because like Jake he refused to take his medications making him extremely violent and unpredictable.

Darren made adult friends and they gave him the wrong advise about not listening to his father. They would entertain all Darren's needs so that he could clean their premises.

Darren then one Saturday told Robert he is going to a baby shower at that adults place. Rina was thinking why would adults want a boy of fifteen years old at a baby shower? But she did not want to cause a scene and quite frankly she was tired of all the violence in the home as this was going on for two years now. Sunday morning at around three Darren came home and Robert opened the door, Darren was heavily under the influence of alcohol and he didn't care if Robert found out that he was drinking. On the Sunday morning he went out again and came home again under the influence. When Robert spoke to him about it and told him he is under age and not allowed to drink or smoke and that he needs permission to leave the home his reaction became severely threatening and violent. "This is my body, I can do what I want, Fuck the government, Fuck the police." He went on fighting and swearing.

Darren was also admitted for the seventy two hour observation on a previous occasion but they refused to admit him stating they have no beds available, however later was found when children is this violent they don't want to admit them.

Rina pleaded with Department SOCIAL development to intervene with Darren as he was busy self destructing and causing a lot of problems. But there was constant excuses why they can't assist. Rina then called the social workers manager to ask her for assistance her reply was shocking "I will not take this matter to children's court without a criminal case number." Rina then approached the children's court for assistance as she knew Darren needed urgent help before he ends up like Jake on the streets drunk and drugged. Rina told the Magistrate at children's court that Department SOCIAL development can't or won't assist without a criminal case number and the police refuse to open criminal charges against the child due to him having mental conditions. The senior Magistrate at children's court then told Rina to get a protection order in place against the child as Darren already strangled Rina before and threatened to stab her thru the ribs when she sleeps, Darren also threatened that he will slit Rina's daughters throat and Jakes throat during the night and drink their blood.

Rina then had no other option than to get the protection order to get Darren the help he needed. Within a week Darren violated the protection order. The police still wanted to stop Rina from opening the case stating they need a warrant of arrest. Rina then went and got the warrant of arrest, while in the police station the officer taking the charge was arrogant and made Rina feel like a criminal. The charge was laid for violation of a court order on a first account and Darren was sent to Secure Care trail awaiting. Up to date Darren is still trail awaiting as the Criminal Justice system enquires a criminal capacity to be done. Its three months after his arrest and still no criminal intend was done or provided.

The reason for this charge was not intended to condemn the child it was done to get him constructive help like with Shane. But now time is getting lost while the child is placed within a "Juvenile " awaiting trail. Darren is sixteen years old there is only two years left to try and reverse this severe behaviour before he is a adult and nothing more can be done.

Olivia stayed in the children's home as prescribed by the court order, she went for one counselling session where it was found that her mental age is to young to receive any kind of therapy as she can't take active part in therapy. The social worker went to court and extended her court order for another two years.

Chapter 4: Conduct Disorder Explained

"**What Are Conduct Disorders?**

Conduct disorder refers to a group of behavioral and emotional problems characterized by a disregard for others. Children with conduct disorder have a difficult time following rules and behaving in a socially acceptable way. Their behavior can be hostile and sometimes physically violent.

In their earlier years, they may show early signs of aggression, including pushing, hitting and biting others. Adolescents and teens with conduct disorder may move into more serious behaviour's, including bullying, hurting animals, picking fights, theft, vandalism and arson.

Children with conduct disorder can be found across all races, cultures and socioeconomic groups. They often have other mental health issues as well that may contribute to the development of the conduct disorder. The disorder is more prevalent in boys than girls.

What Symptoms Should Parents Look for?

There are four basic types of behavior that characterize conduct disorder:

Physical aggression (such as cruelty toward animals, assault or rape).

Violating others' rights (such as theft or vandalism).

Lying or manipulation.

Delinquent behaviour's (such as truancy or running away from home).

Conduct disorder is characterized by aggression toward others and a callous disregard for their rights and needs. Adolescents and teens with conduct disorder can find acts of aggression, deceit and coercion to be gratifying. Your child may meet the criteria for conduct disorder if you find them engaging in several of the below behaviour's:

Bullying or threatening behavior

Physical aggression

Cruelty toward people or animals

Fire-setting

Breaking curfew

Truancy from home or school

Trespassing

Lying

Cheating

Stealing

Vandalism

Emotionally or physically abusive behaviour's (such as wielding a deadly weapon or forcing sex)

Many young people with conduct disorder will have trouble:

Feeling and expressing empathy or remorse.

Showing emotion toward others.

Performing well in the school or community and blaming others for poor performance.

They often misinterpret the actions of others as being hostile or aggressive. They respond by escalating the situation into verbal or physical conflict.

In adolescents and teens, conduct disorder may be associated with other difficulties, including:

Substance use.

Risk-taking behavior.

School problems.

Physical injury from accidents or fights.

In younger children, it can be more of a challenge to distinguish signs of conduct disorder from more typical "acting out".

At times, these same symptoms can be seen in children without the disorder. The difference is frequency, intensity, and duration, as well as to what extent it impacts their functioning. In children with conduct disorder, these behaviour's happen much more frequently.

What Causes Conduct Disorder in Children?

Many factors seem to contribute to this disorder. Research has found that children and teens with conduct disorder seem to have an impairment in the frontal lobe of the brain. This interferes with their ability to plan, avoid harm, and learn from negative experiences.

In addition, these factors seem to put children and teens at a higher risk to develop conduct disorder:

Having experienced abuse, parental rejection or neglect.

Being diagnosed with other psychiatric disorders.

Biological parents diagnosed with ADHD, alcohol use disorder, depression, bipolar disorder, or schizophrenia.

Poor nutrition.

Living in poverty.

Maternal psychopathology.

Poor parenting / lack of parental involvement.

Inconsistent, overly harsh, or otherwise ineffective discipline.

Exposure to violence.

Peer delinquency.

Having been subjected to physical, sexual, and/or emotional abuse.

Lack of adequate parental or other adult supervision.

How Is Conduct Disorder Diagnosed and Treated?

A child psychiatrist, psychologist, or other qualified mental health professional usually diagnoses conduct disorders in children and teens by completing:

A detailed history of the child's behavior, as well as relevant biological, psychological, social, and cultural factors, which are identified during a clinical interview with the child and caregiver(s).

A review of historical data such as school records, court/child welfare records, past treatment records, and interviews with collaterals.

Additional information can also be obtained via the following:

Observations of the child's behavior.

Psychological testing.

Treatment can be complex and challenging. And it can last for several months. Children with conduct disorder tend to be uncooperative with others. They often fear and distrust adults. And adding to the complication is the fact that conduct disorder is often (but not always) diagnosed along with a number of other psychological conditions.

Treatment for conduct disorder may include:

Multisystem therapy: Intensive, often home- or community-based interventions to promote positive behavior change in the youth's environment. Treatment relies heavily on family and school involvement.

Family therapy.

Medication.

Conduct disorder can be difficult to overcome. But it is manageable. The earlier the treatment is started after symptoms appear, the more successful it is likely to be.

As with many psychiatric disorders, early intervention is key"

Chapter 5: Bi Polar Explained

"Bipolar disorder, formerly called manic depression, is a mental health condition that causes extreme mood swings. These include emotional highs, also known as mania or hypomania, and lows, also known as depression. Hypomania is less extreme than mania.

When you become depressed, you may feel sad or hopeless and lose interest or pleasure in most activities. When your mood shifts to mania or hypomania, you may feel very excited and happy (euphoric), full of energy or unusually irritable. These mood swings can affect sleep, energy, activity, judgment, behavior and the ability to think clearly.

Episodes of mood swings from depression to mania may occur rarely or multiple times a year. Each bout usually lasts several days. Between episodes, some people have long periods of emotional stability. Others may frequently have mood swings from depression to mania or both depression and mania at the same time.

Although bipolar disorder is a lifelong condition, you can manage your mood swings and other symptoms by following a treatment plan. In most cases, healthcare professionals use medicines and talk therapy, also known as psychotherapy, to treat bipolar disorder.

Being unusually talkative and talking fast.

Having racing thoughts or jumping quickly from one topic to another.

Being easy to distract.

Making poor decisions. For example, you may go on buying sprees, take sexual risks or make foolish investments.

Major depressive episode

A major depressive episode includes symptoms that are severe enough to cause you to have a hard time doing day-to-day activities. These activities include going to work or school, as well as taking part in social activities and getting along with others.

An episode includes five or more of these symptoms:

Having a depressed mood. You may feel sad, empty, hopeless or tearful. Children and teens who are depressed can seem irritable, angry or hostile.

Having a marked loss of interest or feeling no pleasure in all or most activities.

Losing a lot of weight when not dieting or overeating and gaining weight. When children don't gain weight as expected, this can be a sign of depression.

Sleeping too little or too much.

Feeling restless or acting slower than usual.

Being very tired or losing energy.

Feeling worthless, feeling too guilty or feeling guilty when it's not necessary.

Having a hard time thinking or concentrating, or not being able to make decisions.

Thinking about, planning or attempting suicide.

Other features of bipolar disorder

Symptoms of bipolar disorders, including depressive episodes, may include other features, such as:

Anxious distress, when you're feeling symptoms of anxiety and fear that you're losing control.

Melancholy, when you feel very sad and have a deep loss of pleasure.

Psychosis, when your thoughts or emotions disconnect from reality.

The timing of symptoms may be described as:

Mixed, when you have symptoms of depression and mania or hypomania at the same time.

Rapid cycling, when you have four mood episodes in the past year where you switch between mania and hypomania and major depression.

Also, bipolar symptoms may happen when you're pregnant. Or symptoms can change with the seasons.

Symptoms in children and teens

Symptoms of bipolar disorder can be hard to identify in children and teens. It's often hard to tell whether these symptoms are the usual ups and downs or due to stress or trauma, or if they're signs of a mental health problem other than bipolar disorder.

Children and teens may have distinct major depressive or manic or hypomanic episodes. But the pattern can vary from adults with bipolar disorder. Moods can shift fast during episodes. Some children may have periods without mood symptoms between episodes.

The most noticeable signs of bipolar disorder in children and teenagers may be severe mood swings that aren't like their usual mood swings.

When to see a doctor

Despite their mood extremes, people with bipolar disorder often don't know how much being emotionally unstable disrupts their lives and the lives of their loved ones. As a result, they don't get the treatment they need.

If you're like some people with bipolar disorder, you may enjoy the feelings of euphoria and cycles of being more productive. But an emotional crash always follows this euphoria. This crash can leave you depressed and worn out. It could cause you to have problems getting along with others. It also could leave you in financial or legal trouble.

If you have any symptoms of depression or mania, see your healthcare or mental health professional. Bipolar disorder doesn't get better on its own. A mental health professional with experience in bipolar disorder can help you get your symptoms under control."

https://www.mayoclinic.org/diseases-conditions/ bipolar-disorder/symptoms-causes/syc-20355955

Chapter 6: ADHD Explained

Attention-Deficit/Hyperactivity Disorder

What is ADHD?

Attention-deficit/hyperactivity disorder (ADHD) is marked by an ongoing pattern of inattention and/or hyperactivity-impulsivity that interferes with functioning or development. People with ADHD experience an ongoing pattern of the following types of symptoms:

Inattention means a person may have difficulty staying on task, sustaining focus, and staying organized, and these problems are not due to defiance or lack of comprehension.

Hyperactivity means a person may seem to move about constantly, including in situations when it is not appropriate, or excessively fidgets, taps, or talks. In adults, hyperactivity may mean extreme restlessness or talking too much.

Impulsivity means a person may act without thinking or have difficulty with self-control. Impulsivity could also include a desire for immediate rewards or the inability to delay gratification. An impulsive person may interrupt others or make important decisions without considering long-term consequences.

Attention-Deficit/Hyperactivity Disorder

What is ADHD?

Attention-deficit/hyperactivity disorder (ADHD) is marked by an ongoing pattern of inattention and/or hyperactivity-impulsivity that interferes with functioning or development. People with ADHD experience an ongoing pattern of the following types of symptoms:

◇ **Inattention** means a person may have difficulty staying on task, sustaining focus, and staying organized, and these problems are not due to defiance or lack of comprehension.

◇ **Hyperactivity** means a person may seem to move about constantly, including in situations when it is not appropriate, or excessively fidgets, taps, or talks. In adults, hyperactivity may mean extreme restlessness or talking too much.

◇ **Impulsivity** means a person may act without thinking or have difficulty with self-control. Impulsivity could also include a desire for immediate rewards or the inability to delay gratification. An impulsive person may interrupt others or make important decisions without considering long-term consequences.

What are the signs and symptoms of ADHD?

Some people with ADHD mainly have symptoms of inattention. Others mostly have symptoms of hyperactivity-impulsivity. Some people have both types of symptoms.

Many people experience some inattention, unfocused motor activity, and impulsivity, but for people with ADHD, these behaviour's:

◇ Are more severe

◇ Occur more often

◇ Interfere with or reduce the quality of how they function socially, at school, or in a job

Inattention

People with symptoms of inattention may often:

⬦ Overlook or miss details and make seemingly careless mistakes in schoolwork, at work, or during other activities

⬦ Have difficulty sustaining attention during play or tasks, such as conversations, lectures, or lengthy reading

⬦ Not seem to listen when spoken to directly

⬦ Find it hard to follow through on instructions or finish schoolwork, chores, or duties in the workplace, or may start tasks but lose focus and get easily side tracked

⬦ Have difficulty organizing tasks and activities, doing tasks in sequence, keeping materials and belongings in order, managing time, and meeting deadlines

⬦ Avoid tasks that require sustained mental effort, such as homework, or for teens and older adults, preparing reports, completing forms, or reviewing lengthy papers

⬦ Lose things necessary for tasks or activities, such as school supplies, pencils, books, tools, wallets, keys, paperwork, eyeglasses, and cell phones

⬦ Be easily distracted by unrelated thoughts or stimuli

⬦ Be forgetful in daily activities, such as chores, errands, returning calls, and keeping appointments

Hyperactivity-impulsivity

People with symptoms of hyperactivity-impulsivity may often:

⬦ Fidget and squirm while seated

⬦ Leave their seats in situations when staying seated is expected, such as in the classroom or the office

⬦ Run, dash around, or climb at inappropriate times or, in teens and adults, often feel restless

⬦ Be unable to play or engage in hobbies quietly

⬦ Be constantly in motion or on the go, or act as if driven by a motor

⬦ Talk excessively

⬦ Answer questions before they are fully asked, finish other people's sentences, or speak without waiting for a turn in a conversation

⬦ Have difficulty waiting one's turn

⬦ Interrupt or intrude on others, for example in conversations, games, or activities

Primary care providers sometimes diagnose and treat ADHD. They may also refer individuals to a mental health professional, such as a psychiatrist or clinical psychologist, who can do a thorough evaluation and make an ADHD diagnosis.

For a person to receive a diagnosis of ADHD, the symptoms of inattention and/or hyperactivity-impulsivity must be chronic or long-lasting, impair the person's functioning, and cause the person to fall behind typical development for their age. Stress, sleep disorders, anxiety, depression, and other physical conditions or illnesses can cause similar symptoms to those of ADHD. Therefore, a thorough evaluation is necessary to determine the cause of the symptoms.

Most children with ADHD receive a diagnosis during the elementary school years. For an adolescent or adult to receive a diagnosis of ADHD, the symptoms need to have been present before age 12.

ADHD symptoms can appear as early as between the ages of 3 and 6 and can continue through adolescence and adulthood. Symptoms of ADHD can be mistaken for emotional or disciplinary problems or missed entirely in children who primarily have symptoms of inattention, leading to a delay in diagnosis. Adults with undiagnosed ADHD may have a history of poor academic performance, problems at work, or difficult or failed relationships.

ADHD symptoms can change over time as a person ages. In young children with ADHD, hyperactivity-impulsivity is the most predominant symptom. As a child reaches elementary school, the symptom of inattention may become more prominent and cause the child to struggle academically. In adolescence, hyperactivity seems to lessen and symptoms may more likely include feelings of restlessness or fidgeting, but inattention and impulsivity may remain. Many adolescents with ADHD also struggle with relationships and antisocial behaviour's. Inattention, restlessness, and impulsivity tend to persist into adulthood.

What are the risk factors of ADHD?

Researchers are not sure what causes ADHD, although many studies suggest that genes play a large role. Like many other disorders, ADHD probably results from a combination of factors. In addition to genetics, researchers are looking at possible environmental factors that might raise the risk of developing ADHD and are studying how brain injuries, nutrition, and social environments might play a role in ADHD.

ADHD is more common in males than females, and females with ADHD are more likely to primarily have inattention symptoms. People with ADHD often have other conditions, such as learning disabilities, anxiety disorder, conduct disorder, depression, and substance use disorder.

How is ADHD treated?

While there is no cure for ADHD, currently available treatments may reduce symptoms and improve functioning. Treatments include medication, psychotherapy, education or training, or a combination of treatments.

Medication

For many people, ADHD medications reduce hyperactivity and impulsivity and improve their ability to focus, work, and learn. Sometimes several different medications or dosages must be tried before finding the right one that works for a particular person. Anyone taking medications must be monitored closely by their prescribing doctor.

Stimulants. The most common type of medication used for treating ADHD is called a "stimulant." Although it may seem unusual to treat ADHD with a medication that is considered a stimulant, it works by increasing the brain chemicals dopamine and norepinephrine, which play essential roles in thinking and attention.

Under medical supervision, stimulant medications are considered safe. However, like all medications, they can have side effects, especially when misused or taken in excess of the prescribed dose, and require an individual's health care provider to monitor how they may be reacting to the medication.

Non-stimulants. A few other ADHD medications are non-stimulants. These medications take longer to start working than stimulants, but can also improve focus, attention, and impulsivity in a person with ADHD. Doctors may prescribe a non-stimulant: when a person has bothersome side effects from stimulants, when a stimulant was not effective, or in combination with a stimulant to increase effectiveness.

Although not approved by the U.S. Food and Drug Administration (FDA) specifically for the treatment of ADHD, some antidepressants are used alone or in combination with a stimulant to treat ADHD. Antidepressants may help all of the symptoms of ADHD and can be prescribed if a patient has bothersome side effects from stimulants. Antidepressants can be helpful in combination with stimulants if a patient also has another condition, such as an anxiety disorder, depression, or another mood disorder. Non-stimulant ADHD medications and antidepressants may also have side effects.

Doctors and patients can work together to find the best medication, dose, or medication combination. To find the latest information about medications, talk to a health care provider and visit the FDA website ."

https://www.nimh.nih.gov/health/topics/attention-deficit-hyperactivity-disorder-adhd

Chapter 6: Revelations

Over a two year period while the boys were home Rina did follow up investigations into the removal, the court proceedings, the abuse and the places where the children was placed for the seven years they were in the welfare system. And the following discoveries was made and found.

The children individually told Rina everything that occurred in the first place where they were placed, the place of safety. It was cross checked with other children coming from the same place of safety and most of the stories was confirmed. This chapter is to reveal the real things that happens in places of safety, children's homes and secure centres.

Place of Safety North of Pretoria:

1.Children received physical discipline by the owner or she would call her son to come and "discipline " the children. This was done by breaking a wooden hair brush on one child's head. Beating another one with a belt over his back and legs that left blue marks on him.

2. Children was used to do labour on farms and venues

3. Children was shouted and sweared at

4. Olivia was molested and raped and when Shane reported it he was beaten by the owner telling him he is lying although the same owner laid a charge against Jake for rape on his sister Olivia. That was only found out after the boys was already re unified.

5. Olivia being thrown with a scissor in the face by the owner.

6. Parental alienation.

7. Calling Jake snake

8. Drowning the children in the swimming pool and just before they stop breathing bring them up slap them and dunk their heads back in the water.

9. Co hersing older kids to beat the younger ones until they bleed and then leave them with bloody clothes.

10. Placing videos and photos of the children's faces on social media and YouTube for donations, not covering the children's faces.

When Rina checked the Place of Safety registration documents she found that this institution was not registered as a place of safety and neither were they registered at the Department of Social Development as the law states they should be to operate. Rina immediately gave statements of all children involved to the Department of Social Development to stop any registration process because of this severe allegations, she wanted them to investigate this place properly. Because of the case of Robert and several other cases that was brought to the Department of Social Development by other child activists and parents a massive investigation was on the way for all NPO welfare organisations. Department of Social Development took two thousand files to start the investigations. Rina wanted to assist with this exposure of this NPO organisations and unregistered places so she did extensive background checks and provided feedback to the Department of Social Development as she got any information.

"All Child and Youth Care Centres must be registered

11 May 2021

- ◇
- ◇
- ◇

Listen[1]

All Child and Youth Care Centres (CYCCs) are required to be registered with the provincial Department of Social Development (DSD).

A Child and Youth Care Centre (CYCC) is a facility that provides a form of alternative care for children outside of the family environment. Children under the age of 18 years old, who are living and working on the streets, are urged to seek accommodation at child and youth care centres that provide specialised programmes and are registered with the provincial DSD

"It is illegal for any facility to provide accommodation to children without being registered.

I wish to urge all members of the public, to check on the registration status of the facility or organisation, offering accommodation for children. By doing this, you can help ensure that children in need of care and protection are placed at a facility where they will be treated with respect and that their human rights are protected," said the Western Cape Minister of Social Development, Sharna Fernandez.

The Children's Act (38 of 2005) ensures that children that are living on the streets, or are not safe at home or in their communities can be placed in alternative care. This process is coordinated through the Children's Court. In instances where foster care or placement with extended family is not possible, children are placed in a Child and Youth care Centre. It is ultimately the courts right to determine the

---

1.   http://app.readspeaker.com/cgi-bin/
rsent?customerid=7026&lang=en_za&readid=rs_read&url=http%3A%2F%2Fwww.westernca
pe.gov.za%2Fnews%2Fall-child-and-youth-care-centres-must-be-registered

best placement for the child according to the investigation and recommendations of the external social worker's report.

In the Western Cape, there is a total of 53 registered NPO centres and 8 registered DSD managed CYCCs.

For the 2020/21 financial year, R 429. 24 million has been budgeted towards residential alternative care.

CYCCs already funded by the DSD do not need to submit their contact details as we are aware of their services.

The following facilities need to apply for registration:

⬨ Children's Homes are for children who are placed by order of the children's court into short term residential care.

⬨ Temporary Safe Care offers short-term care for both children who have been found in need of care and protection due to abuse, negligence or have been exploited, as well as children who have violated the law and are awaiting trial or an inquiry.

Finding the right accommodation for children:
Consult the list of Child and Youth Care Centres to find the shelter nearest you[2].

Unregistered child and youth care centres (CYCCs):

Unregistered CYCCs may not comply with the prescribed norms and standards, hence people accessing such services should be aware that they run the risk of placing children in an environment where they may have their rights violated, run the risk of injury, even death.

2. https://eur03.safelinks.protection.outlook.com/?url=https%3A%2F%2Fwww.westerncape.gov.za%2Feng%2Fyour_gov%2F4190%2Ffacilities%2F239717&data=04%7C01%7CNikiwe.Vuba%40westerncape.gov.za%7C76f71106970c444574af08d9146a03b0%7Cae74bf7fcfc34760a1fe0731afaa5502%7C0%7C0%7C637563267841816102%7CUnknown%7CTWFpbGZsb3d8eyJWIjoiMC4wLjAwMDAiLCJQIjoiV2luMzIiLCJBTiI6Ik1haWwiLCJXVCI6Mn0%3D%7C1000&sdata=EHsbakSrPty5JIpAZwfoKwz%2F6tHmAs9vQzv6jKJtnA0%3D&reserved=0

Unregistered CYCCs may not have trained staff, expertise or resources to deal with crises and/or complications associated with children in need of care and protection."

https://www.westerncape.gov.za/news/all-child-and-youth-care-centres-must-be-registered

Section 28 of the Bill of Rights, entitled "Children", says:

Every child has the right to –

A name and a nationality from birth;

Family care or parental care, or to appropriate alternative care when removed from the family environment;

Basic nutrition, shelter, basic health care services and social services;

Be protected from maltreatment, neglect, abuse or degradation;

Be protected from exploitative labour practices

Not be required or permitted to perform work or provide services that –

Are inappropriate for a person of that child's age; or

Place at risk the child's well-being, education, physical or mental health or spiritual, moral or social development;

Not be detained except as a measure of last resort, in which case, in addition to the rights a child enjoys under sections 12 and 35, the child may be detained only for the shortest appropriate period of time, and has the right to be –

Kept separately from detained persons over the age of 18 years; and

Is treated in a manner, and kept in conditions, that take account of the child's age;

Have a legal practitioner assigned to the child by the state, and at state expense, in civil proceedings affecting the child, if substantial injustice would otherwise result; and

Not be used directly in armed conflict, and to be protected in times of armed conflict.

A child's best interests are of paramount importance in every matter concerning the child.

In this section 'child' means a person under the age of 18 years.

This section gives children the right to a name, citizenship and some form of care. Children need food and shelter, and should be protected from abuse, neglect and degradation. No child should work when under-age, or do work that would interfere with his or her education or development.

Children should be jailed only as a last resort and should not have to share a cell with adults. They should not take part in wars and should be protected during conflict.

The second sub-section, a very important clause, says a child's interests are the most important consideration in any matter concerning the child."

https://www.concourt.org.za/index.php/children-s-rights

In the words of the children involved:

Hanna: "The welfare removed us like dogs from our parents."

Darren: "The people beat us, I was raped and drowned."

Shane: "The people at social services offices hurt us when we go for assessments."

Jake: "They called me snake and made me wash pig pans, its my fault we were taken by social services."

Rina took all this new found information and reported it to Department of Social Development. But in the end Department SOCIAL Development went ahead and registered this place of safety even after they had all the evidence of abuse.

Regarding the court order that initially placed the children in this place of safety:

The court order was for a period of ninety days that is a three month period. After the ninety days the case was supposed to be reviewed, that never happened. As per law all placements at safe care facilities must be reviewed every two years if not otherwise stated by a court order, this also never happened. So effectively after the removal and ninety days was over the children should have been returned to Robert or a new court order should have been obtained. Because not one of these stipulations was done for four years and nine months this children was in this illegal place of safety without a court order making it "kidnapping".

When the Robert asked for the children to be moved from the place of safety the social worker grabbed the opportunity to get a new court order. That is why they were so keen to go with Robert suggestion. Not because they thought it's a good idea, because they never reviewed the case as per law.

Questions that Rina and Robert asked regarding the place of safety, but never got answers to:

. How could a place of safety operate for so many years without being registered?

. When the abuse with avidavids was send to Department of Social Development, why didn't they do a proper investigation and closed the place down?

. Why didn't Department of Social Development do the form 22 and report this matters to the police service?

. When Hanna wanted to open the Criminal case against the place of safety, why did the police refuse to open a docket? (on this question Robert got the answer from a police official, after the avidavid was given to the social worker, she went to the police station and intimidated the police official.) She did it so good that the official refused to ever speak to Robert again.

. Olivia was apparently raped in the place of safety, by older boys, that was in Shane's statement. However, prove could be found that the place of safety opened a case of rape against Jake. Olivia was never taken for therapy nor is any J88 available for this case. Why was this matter not properly attended to?

. After evidence and numerous statements was given to the relevant department, they still went ahead and registered the place of safety. They are now legally keeping children in their care.

. Is it then safe to say that, the Department who is supposed to investigate and obtain good standings hereby condone abuse and unlawful placements in unregistered places?

. It is the duty and the sole purpose of the Department to ensure all children are safe and that places where this children is placed are safe and registered.

.In this case we can safely say the Department failed the children and lacked to provide the service they were intended for.

Children's home

The children reported numerous beatings especially Shane. Although he is a child with severe mental health and behavioural problems it is out of law to abuse him. This is severely traumatised children and by working with them it should be done in a constructive way. The way the children was handled contributed to the trauma.

Shane-

"The house father picked me up and threw me against the wall, because I was angry and swore at him."

"The aunty jumped on me and strangled me."

"When I'm naughty they locked me in my room, so I broke the window and climbed on top of the roof."

"When I was naughty they gave me pap with salt and vinegar to eat and water, no coffee or tea. The other children could eat nice things but not me."

Jake-

"I got into a fight with another boy, we were hitting each other. The house mother came in between and I accidentally hit her in the face.

She told another big boy to beat me. He broke my nose. I was refused to open a assault charge, they only took me for x rays.

Olivia-

Because Olivia's brain development is severely delayed she can not be asked about everything. But there is sufficient evidence of the following.

.Olivia was raped at the age of nine in the children's home, that can be seen on the J88 that was completed by a medical practitioner.

. Olivia had severe trauma at a very young age that contributed to her developmental delays.

. On one visitation Olivia's hair was lice invested

On one weekend when the boys came home to Robert on a leave of absence, Shane had a severe red rush all over his body. Rina took him to the pharmacy who thought it might me German Measles. The Monday when Shane was back at the children's home the homes social worker made a statement. "Your mother must wash your bedding more frequently, that's why you have the rush, the bedding is dirty." Although Shane came home with the rush. Once again the parents was blamed for something that happened while in the care of a children's home.

It's also during this time that Robert refused to work with the NPO organisation any longer. The NPO went to court and the Magistrates court in Pretoria gave a order for the Department to take over the case file. There was numerous emails send from the NPO to the Department regarding this matter. But the Department refused to take over the case even when a court instructed them to do so.

This placed them in contempt of court, yet nothing was ever done about it. Its only after Rina wrote to Parliament that the Department took over several cases including Robert file.

In the children's home when children are misbehaving the police gets called. One police official a woman standing in the station as a children's officer would then slap the children and threaten them.

Questions about the children's home

In Olivia's case, why was she allowed alone with older boys?

Where was the supervision?

Why is there no camera's in the vicinity?

Why was Jake denied to open assault cases?

When abuse on the children was reported to the social worker at the home and to the NPO social worker, why was this never investigated?

How could a Magistrate not see that there was no valid court order from the Place of safety in the North of Pretoria when they gave a new order to the children's home?

The case of Robert was severe, with no positive outcome. Robert was targeted by this Christian Based NPO social services entities without justification. For almost nineteen years of his life he had to fight constantly for his children that he never did any harm. Tactics and excuses used for this removals and or keeping of his children was unfounded and unlawful. Not just causing severe psychological damage to the children but also had a severe impact on Robert financial, physical, and mental health.

In the next chapter evidence, and law will be combined to show a clear picture of the case and how illegal this case was dealt with. All institutions will be mentioned who had a role in the total destruction of this family. However no names will be mentioned to protect the family from further harassment.

Chapter 7: Failing Institutions

Police:

Hanna wanted to open a abuse case against the Place of safety in the North of Pretoria. She was accompanied by Robert to the police station in their Jurisdiction. The police refused to open the case and only let her do a avidavid.

What does the law say about child abuse?

◇ If there is a suspicion that a child is being abused, it must be reported to the police (where criminal charges can be brought), a designated child protection organisation or to a social worker at the Department of Social Development.

◇ A protection order in South Africa[1] can also be obtained under the Protection from Harassment Act or Domestic Violence Act to prevent a person from abusing a child.

◇ Any person can voluntarily report child abuse. A child can also report child abuse without the assistance of his/her parents, however, it is advisable that a child approach a trusted adult for guidance and assistance.

◇ https://www.legalwise.co.za/help-yourself/legal-articles/child-abuse

---

1. https://www.legalwise.co.za/help-yourself/quicklaw-guides/domestic-violence-protection-orders

The avidavid made by Hanna only the first page to show it's a official police document.

The same police station also refused to open cases against the children who committed crimes, while the neighbours also laid complaints numerous times. The excuses used was that the children is mental health patients they can do nothing. But yet the Criminal Procedures act, states differently.

Section 79 of the Criminal Procedure Act 51 of 1977 provides for the appointment of mental health professionals to assess an accused's fitness to stand trial and/or criminal capacity if the court orders such an enquiry in terms of sections 77 and 78 of the Criminal Procedure Act>.

This shows the total lack of knowledge by the police officials. Rina went to the station commander about this and she showed him this Act as well. His reply "My officers know what to do they are send on regular courses. I can not do anything without a court order."

This police station did not act when the children caused damage to property, assault, placed themselves and others in danger. They did not act when one child stabbed another one with a knife, they did not act when other parents wanted to lay Criminal charges for the assault on their child in school.

After Rina told this police officials many times that the children has behavioural problems that's why they get medications from a mental institution, the officials still did not comply to law.

On another occasion the constables who was called to assist in getting Darren home from neighbours, who did not have the authority or the permission from the Father to have Darren there. This constables went and gave the minor child of fifteen the right to be were he wants to be without parental consent

This made the already volatile situation worse as now the child believed he could do whatever he wanted. And that his father has no say whatsoever.

The Children's Act, 38 of 2005

The Children's Act, 38 of 2005, is a legal document that regulates all aspects relating to children. The Children's Act covers a variety of aspects relating to children, including giving effect to certain rights of children as provided for in the Constitution; providing for children in so far as their care and protection is concerned; defining parental responsibilities and rights of parents; and a number of additional aspects.

For purposes of this article, and specifically, to deal with the aspect of parental responsibilities and rights, we will consider Section 18, contained under Chapter 3 of the Children's Act.

Section 18 of the Children's Act sets out in detail the meaning of parental responsibilities and rights. Section 18(2) provides that parental responsibilities and rights which a person may have in respect of a child include the responsibility and right to: –

To care for the child;

(b) to maintain contact with the child;

© to act as guardian of the child; and

(d) to contribute towards the maintenance of the child.

The Department of Social Development created a booklet which explains the rights of children, as well as the responsibilities and rights of parents, and can be found here.

The Responsibility to Care for the child

Each parent has a responsibility to care for their child. This means that each parent has a responsibility to provide their child with a suitable place to live; living conditions that are conducive to the child's health, well-being and development; and the necessary financial support.

Caring for a child also means, inter alia, safeguarding and promoting the well-being of the child; protecting the child from maltreatment; guarding against any infringements of the child's rights; guiding, directing and securing the child's education; guiding the child's behaviour in a humane manner; maintaining a sound relationship with the child, and ensuring that the best interests of the child is the paramount concern in all matters affecting the child.

Parents should also ensure that their children are safe and secure at all times, which includes monitoring what they do online and keeping an eye on who they associate with. Parents also have a responsibility to teach their children how to be responsible citizens.

https://pagelschulenburg.co.za/understanding-your-parental-responsibilities-and-rights-in-south-africa/

Once again Robert ́s responsibility as a parent was not taken into account, the safe keeping of his child. And this by police officials who should abide by the law just like any other citizen.

Christian Based NPO Social Welfare Organisation:

Social workers made statements that Robert severely abused his children by beating them blue. This statements was on record in court files. However no prove to these allegations was ever produced. Assessments done on the children was done by a woman who works within the organisation.

In the initial assessments it's stated that the children was abused by Robert. However no criminal charges was laid, no J88 forms are on record and no form 22 was filled out.

Bringing to the conclusion that this statements and assessments was fabricated for a purpose to remove the children from their family home.

Justice through the J88: The doctor's role in the criminal justice system

To the Editor: South Africa has an unacceptably high rate of interpersonal violence.1 Recent well-publicised incidents have prompted South Africans to re-examine the massive problem of violence against women in the country.2 As healthcare practitioners, many South African doctors are regularly exposed to victims of violent crime and are responsible for their care. For those victims who wish to make a case, the J88 form serves as a crucial piece of medical evidence.3 It is an official form issued by the Department of Justice which documents the medico-legal examination that the healthcare practitioner performs on a victim and highlights findings that are potentially relevant for legal purposes. It is not clear how aware doctors are of the importance of timely, thorough and accurate completion of the J88 form.

Final-year medical students at Stellenbosch University, Western Cape, South Africa, spend their Community Health and Family Medicine rotation in groups at primary care facilities. At a community health centre (CHC) in Cape Town, the medical manager brought a perceived problem concerning the management of assault victims who wish to make a case to the attention of the students allocated there.

The problem was related to the protocol for obtaining, completion and further management of the J88 form. There seems to be a lack of clarity concerning each party's role in the process, which sometimes results in the victim terminating the case before completion. The student group decided to tackle this issue by performing a quality improvement cycle at the CHC and developing a standard operating procedure for the doctors working in casualty to follow.

Not only are the logistics of the J88 form important; how the doctor fills in the form is also critical. The content of the form should be of the highest quality in terms of accuracy and thoroughness. A training session on how to fill in each section correctly was hosted for the doctors at the CHC. (The need for training of locum doctors still exists, as the after-hours trauma services are covered by locum staff for a third of the time.) The Forensic Medicine Department at Stellenbosch University has also agreed to include training on the J88 during the 'wound description' lectures in the undergraduate forensics course. Current and future doctors need to be equipped with the knowledge and skills necessary to fill in the J88 form. Most importantly, doctors need to adopt a willing attitude and make themselves available to help.

This small project revealed an important gap in medical education and practice. Research is needed to delineate the problem and determine its extent. Barriers to the completion of J88 forms should be identified and actively addressed. It is essential that all the parties involved are aware of their specific roles in the process, and policy should be formulated to clarify these roles. As doctors, we need to remember that we play a vital part in ensuring that justice is served in cases of assault and rape, and we should take our role in the process seriously. Healthcare practitioners have an obligation not only to individual patients, but also to society as a whole.4 Let us join the fight against violence and work for 'justice through the J88'.

http://www.samj.org.za/index.php/samj/article/view/7084/5188

Robert never received a copy of the removal form or the court order, and did not know the charges against him, or the reasons to the removal of his children. As the law states that you have the right to know what is said about you and what is on official documents were your name is used in a court of law. You have the right to defend yourself from allegations. The Christian Based NPO social workers refused to make this documents available to Robert.

Section 32 – Access to information. This section, entitled, "Access to information", says: Everyone has the right of access to any information held by the state; and any information that is held by another person and that is required for the exercise or protection of any rights.

This fabrication of events that never took place made the NPO liable for perjury cases.

Perjury: the offence of wilfully telling an untruth or making a misrepresentation under oath.

This may not seem that serious or impossible to affect the everyday person, but it can take on many forms and is more common than one may think.

In a South African context perjury cases can be prosecuted against anyone who lays criminal charges – opens a police case or files an affidavit – claiming a crime has taken place which is not entirely the truth.

Opening of any police cases for investigation is considered statement under oath.

Lying under oath makes you guilty of a crime

Perjury: the offence of wilfully telling an untruth or making a misrepresentation under oath.

This may not seem that serious or impossible to affect the everyday person, but it can take on many forms and is more common than one may think.

In a South African context perjury cases can be prosecuted against anyone who lays criminal charges – opens a police case or files an affidavit – claiming a crime has taken place which is not entirely the truth.

Opening of any police cases for investigation is considered statement under oath.

A second aspect relates to witness testimony in a court of law or during a criminal investigation. Should the person not be honest during the process, perjury charges could be brought against them, so their lie is punishable by law.

Perjury cases have also been brought against some government and political heavy hitters in recent years, such as ANC Women's League head Bathabile Dlamini this year.

The Gauteng courts heard a motion to charge her with perjury following her testimony during an inquiry the Constitutional Court had instituted into her role in the 2017 social grants crisis while she was still serving as a cabinet minister.

Also this year charges were brought against Public Protector Busisiwe Mkhwebane, who was accused of lying under oath in November 2017 when she, according to News24, "unlawfully and intentionally deposed to an answering affidavit under oath in a Gauteng High Court review application."

https://www.news24.com/news24/community-newspaper/ peoples-post/lying-under-oath-makes-you-guilty-of-a-crime- 20211025-2

The same NPO used illegal forms to remove the children from their family home. Stating the children is in need of care and protection. Although the form 36 section 151/152 was found unconstitutional in 2012 in the High Court or Pretoria, this social workers still used this form in 2015 to remove Robert children.

https://www.saflii.org/za/cases/ZACC/2012/1.html

Children's Act: Constitutional Court Judgment: Invalidity of sections 151/152: Child can be removed from family and placed in temporary safe care, but no provision for child to be brought before children's court for automatic review of removal

https://www.gov.za/documents/notices/childrens-act-constitutional-court-judgment-invalidity-sections-151152-child-can

The NPO had a court order for a ninety day period to do a proper investigation on the family circumstances and have the case reviewed. This never happened. The case was not reviewed for a further four years and nine months. That said, the children was kept at the Pretoria North Place of Safety without a valid court order. This made the placement illegal.

When can a child leave the foster care household?

Generally a child can leave alternative care at the age of 18. An alternative

Care order usually lapses after two years or a shorter period if so ordered and

The court may then extend the order for two years at a time. However when it

Comes to foster care placements the court can rule that the order subsists until

The child reaches 18. If the child was placed with a family member the court

Can rule that the order extends for more then two years at a time.

If a court ordered the foster placement to subsist until the child turns 18 then

The child will not be able to leave the foster household until the age of 18

Unless a court terminates the foster care before the child turns 18. If a court did

Not order that the foster care placement runs until the child is 18, that foster

Child is still entitled (but not obliged) to remain in foster care until the age of

18. Furthermore, a child will also be able to remain in foster care until the age

Of 21 in order to complete his/her education if the foster parents agree to this

And are able to care for the child until then.

The foster parent may also grant the foster child a leave of absence allowing

Him/her to be away from the foster parent or household under certain

Conditions, but the child cannot leave the country without authorisation from

The provincial head of social development.

Conclusion

Foster care placements are not meant to be permanent and it does not dissolve the

Parental rights and responsibilities of biological parents towards their child (unless a

Court made an order to that effect), but it is aimed at providing children in need of

Care and protection with a stable, safe and healthy environment and to promote

Permanency planning for that child's future. Given the need to provide stable and

Permanent homes for the thousands of desperate and vulnerable children in the

Country, foster care placement is encouraged and legal professionals must be equipped

To readily advice clients on process and procedure to secure the best possible

Outcomes for children in need of foster homes.

The abuse, degradation, humiliation by the Place of Safety was reported to the NPO social workers yet they did nothing to get the children safe. This abuse was also evident on emotional assessments done on the children before the re unification.

What happens if a child is seriously injured/ abused or dies while in foster Care?

If the child has been abused or seriously injured, the foster parent must

Immediately report this to the provincial head of social development who must

Investigate the circumstances of the injury or abuse.

Section 178 does not

Address the situation of who should report if it is the foster parent who could

Have been responsible for the injury or the abuse and they withhold this

Information. This situation is covered by section 110 of the Act that requires

Members of certain professions (like social workers, doctors and teachers) to

Report abuse to the provincial department of social development, a designated

Child protection organisation or a police official. Furthermore, any person who

This is important to note since it is an exception to section 129 of the Act which does not allow care givers to consent to a child's surgery.

Section 178 of the Act.

Suspects that a child is being abused may also report it to a social worker or

The police.

If the fostered child dies this must also be reported by the foster parent to the

Child's parents/guardian (if they can be traced); a police official; the provincial

Head of social development and a social worker. The police official must

Investigate the child's death unless he or she is satisfied that the child died of

Natural causes. It is an offence not to report serious injury, abuse, neglect or

Death of a child in foster care and a person convicted could face a fine or

Imprisonment of 10 years or both.

https://centreforchildlaw.co.za/wordpress21/wp-content/uploads/2019/02/issue22.pdf

This NPO organisation social workers also questioned the integrity of the family as well as discriminated against the living circumstances of the family. And used any and all they could to not do the re unification. On one of the reports that was admitted to court the social worker mentioned that the family uses solar electricity that's illegal. Since when is solar electricity illegal?

There was instinctive investigations on the financial stability of the family. Even Rina who at that point was not married to Robert and who is not the biological parent was investigated. Reports were found where the NPO Social worker checked if Rina received any

Government Funding (Sassa grant). They did not have Rina's permission to investigate her private life or affairs.

The case was not against Rina, she had no bloodlines with the family involved and she was not married to Robert at that time.

https://www.justice.gov.za/constitution/chp02.html

Department of Social Development:

During the transition from the Place of Safety to the Children's home, a court order was given that the Department should take over the case from the NPO. Numerous emails regarding this was send from the NPO to the Department. The Department replied on that emails but did not proceed to take over the case. Placing them in contempt of court.

Should you simply choose to ignore a court order, you may be held in contempt of court. Your action of disobedience will be seen as interference with the administration of justice by lowering the respect and authority of the court, which may be punishable as a criminal offence. An application must be made to the court to hold you in contempt of an order. Our Constitutional Court has listed certain requirements that must be proved beyond a reasonable doubt before a contempt of court application may succeed.

The existence of a valid court order;

The Court Order must have been brought to the attention of the alleged contemnor;

There must be a form of non-compliance with the court order; and

The non-compliance must be wilful and/or intentional.

If the above elements are present, an Order to place you in contempt may be granted against you which is punishable by a fine and/or imprisonment.

https://www.bbplaw.attorney/refuse-to-comply-with-court-order/

Before Rina wrote to the Parliament about this case she contacted the Department of Social Development for help and intervention. She send them all the documents and proof she could find. However after two days she was told by the Department they can do nothing as it is a ongoing court case. All this while the children was severely abused within the welfare system.

Social Development

Official Guide to South AfricaThe Department of Social Development (DSD) provides social protection services and leads government's efforts to forge partnerships through which vulnerable individuals, groups and communities become capable and active participants in the development of themselves and society.

The social development function facilitates access to social grants and welfare services to reduce poverty and inequality, protect children, and empower women, youth and people with disabilities.

https://www.gov.za/about-sa/social-development

The Department of Social Development was well aware that the Place of Safety was not fully registered as numerous child activists reported it to them, including Rina. However they did not close the place down or remove the children from that place. Instead they took another two years to register the place where child abuse was evident.

Department of Social Development who obviously neglected their duties and indirectly caused this children to be abused within the welfare system did nothing to prevent this from happening again.

Children's Courts

During court proceedings, Robert was never allowed to give his side of the story or to defend himself. In one specific court hearing the Magistrate actually told him straight out to keep quite. The children's court does not come across family friendly. Some Magistrates listen to every word the social worker speaks even calls the social worker "my soldiers out there."

Why didn't the court make sure the Place of Safety is registered before placing the children in their care?

Why was no contempt of court ever filed against Department of Social Development who disobeyed a court order?

How could the court not see that a court order lapsed almost five years before? And just grant a new order without a proper investigation report?

How can a children's court except illegal removal documents and make a decision and order without justifiable cause?

Looking at just a few of the "mistakes" from various departments that caused life long negative effects on numerous people, the following was observed.

Not one of the above mentioned institutions wants to take any responsibility for their actions. They keep blaming each other and passing the problem.

In the meantime five children's life's was disrupted severely. The psychological effects on four of them is so severe that they have to be institutionalised to try and remedy some of the effects of severe trauma.

While this same institutions still go about their daily lives this family will never fully recover from this extremely sad event.

There are numerous other families going thru the same ordeal and nowhere they turn is any help available. Because it seems like every institution or organisation that's there to protect the most vulnerable fails them miserably.

In this case the passing of the problem went from:

NPO welfare to

Department Social Development

After this the family needed urgent assistance with the rehabilitation of the children due to trauma caused within the system.

Department Social Development made it a problem for Police and Police refusing cases made it the problem of Mental Institutions.

Mental Institutions clearly stated that the children is accounted for their behaviour and should face the consequences accordingly.

Children's court with Department of Social Development made it the problem the for the Justice System. Because social development refused placement for a troubled child without a criminal case. But when the criminal case eventually was opened the same Department closed the child's file stating. "We are closing the file, it's now out of our hands." Now this child is stuck in the criminal justice system when he actually just needed a secure place with strict rules and extensive counselling.

Chapter 8: Cases and Media Reports

South Africa: North Gauteng High Court, Pretoria

You are here: SAFLII >> Databases >> South Africa: North Gauteng High Court, Pretoria >> 2023 >> [2023] ZAGPPHC 47

| Noteup | LawCite

Christelike Maatskaplike Raad Noord ("CMR North") v Department of Social Development and Others (32944/2022) [2023] ZAGPPHC 47 (3 February 2023)

Download original files

PDF format

RTF format

IN THE HIGH COURT OF SOUTH AFRICA

(GAUTENG DIVISION, PRETORIA)

CASE NO: 32944/2022

(1)REPORTABLE: NO

(2) OF INTEREST TO OTHER JUDGES: NO

(3) REVISED: NO

DATE: 3 FEBRUARY 2023

In the application between:

CHRISTELIKE MAATSKAPLIKE RAAD

NOORD ("CMR NORTH") Applicant

And

DEPARTMENT OF SOCIAL DEVELOPMENT First Respondent

MEC FOR THE GAUTENG DEPARTMENT Second Respondent

OF SOCIAL DEVELOPMENT

DIRECTOR-GENERAL, DEPARTMENT OF Third Respondent

SOCIAL DEVELOPMENT

MINISTER OF THE DEPARTMENT OF Fourth Respondent
SOCIAL DEVELOPMENT
VARIOUS INTERVENING PARTIES Amici Curiae
Coram: Millar J
Heard on: 3 February 2023
Delivered: 3 February 2023 – This judgment was handed down electronically by circulation to the parties' representatives by email, by being uploaded to the CaseLines system of the GD and by release to SAFLII. The date and time for hand-down is deemed to be 12h45 on 3 February 2023.
JUDGMENT
MILLAR J

1. This is an application for leave to appeal brought by the first respondent against a judgment and orders granted by me on 20 October 2022. The application for leave to appeal was served out of time on 14 December 2022 and thereafter the next day an application for condonation was served. The application for condonation was not opposed. It is in the interests of justice that this application be heard and so I indicated that I intend to grant condonation.[1]

1. The test for granting leave to appeal The test for the granting of leave to appeal pertinent to the present matter is set out in section 17(1) of the Superior Courts Act[2] as follows:

"(1) Leave to appeal may only be given where the judge or judges concerned are of the opinion that

a. (i) the appeal would have a reasonable prospect of success or

(ii) there is some other compelling reason why the appeal should be heard, including conflicting Judgments on the matter under consideration"

1. I have considered the grounds upon which the application has been brought and the reasons given by me for the judgment. I have also considered the submissions made by counsel for the granting of leave to appeal on the part of the first respondent and those opposing the granting of leave to appeal on behalf of the applicant.

1. I am not persuaded that another court would come to a different conclusion or that there is some other compelling reason why leave to appeal should be granted.

1. Since the application for condonation was not opposed, I do not intend to make any order for costs in regard thereto. The costs order that I make relates solely to the application for leave to appeal. There is no reason to depart from the normal rule that the scale of costs be paid as between party and party.

1. In the circumstances, I make the following order:

6.1 Condonation is granted for the late filing of the application for leave to appeal.

6.2 The application for leave to appeal is refused.

6.3 The first respondent is ordered to pay the costs of the applicant on the scale as between party and party which costs are to include the costs consequent upon the employment of two counsel.

A MILLAR

JUDGE OF THE HIGH COURT
GAUTENG DIVISION, PRETORIA
HEARD ON: 3 FEBRUARY 2023
JUDGMENT DELIVERED ON: 3 FEBRUARY 2023
COUNSEL FOR THE APPLICANTS: ADV. L HAUPT SC
ADV. L VAN DER WESTHUIZEN
INSTRUCTED BY: F VAN WYK INCORPORATED
REFERENCE: MS. A JACOBS

COUNSEL FOR THE 1ST
RESPONDENT: ADV. M BOTMA
INSTRUCTED BY: THE STATE ATTORNEY, PRETORIA
REFERENCE: MR. S MODUKANELE
[1] Ferris v First Rand Bank 2014 (3) SA 39 (CC) at 43G-44A
[2] 10 of 2013

https://maroelamedia.co.za/nuus/sa-nuus/vrou-nooit-gedwing-om-te-lieg-oor-verkragting/[1]

In the following report can be seen where the problem starts.

https://www.timeslive.co.za/news/south-africa/2010-12-09-child-porn-the-excuses/

09 December 2010 2 Min Read

Child porn: the excuses

In News / South Africa by CHANDRÉ PRINCE

Nobody wants to take responsibility for placing two foster children with the family implicated in the country's biggest child-pornography ring.

---

1. https://maroelamedia.co.za/nuus/sa-nuus/vrou-nooit-gedwing-om-te-lieg-oor-verkragting/

The Gauteng Department of Health and Social Development has tried to shift the blame for the placement of a six-year-old boy and an eight-year-old girl onto a non-profit Christian welfare organisation.

The children were removed from the family's Pretoria North plot in March and October. Statements detailing their alleged abuse led to the recent arrest of eight members of the family.

Health department spokesman Mandla Sidu said the Christelike Maatskaplike Raad, not the department, had placed the children in the family's care.

"When the area the plot is in was given back to the department during 2006, the CMR Wonderboom decided to keep this case because the two children were in foster care and it was decided it was not in their interests to be handed over to another organisation," he said.

The girl was placed in foster care in May 2005, the boy in February 2006.

The director of the Christelike Maatskaplike Raad North, Edelweiss Schieke, defended its decision, saying it believed at the time that it was acting in the children's best interests.

"I feel we dealt with it in a responsible way, but everyone is now pointing fingers at us," she said.

Schieke said correct procedures were followed, including the screening of the foster parents.

"Maybe circumstances were not that bad then."

Last week, police, social workers and The Times were shocked by the living conditions at the family's small holdings.

An overpowering stench of dog, cat, pig and human excrement emanated from the rooms of the dilapidated houses.

Schieke said there was a "great shortage" of foster parents and places of safety, and her organisation was often forced to "make do with what we have".

"Where do we go with them? There are not a lot of places."

There was also a dire shortage of social workers, she said. Practising social workers were overburdened. On average, Christelike Maatskaplike Raad social workers had a workload of 150 cases each, and up to 40 court cases pending.

"How on Earth can you do a proper job if we are understaffed and overworked?" she said. Social workers earn about R101000 a year.

Schieke said that, despite the challenges, social workers did their utmost:"We really try to act in the best interests of the children, but people don't know what we deal with."

The social worker currently handling the children's case, who told the police of their plight, is on sick leave: "She is very stressed," Schieke said.

She objected to the formal complaint made by the charity Helping Hand against the social worker who placed the children, who no longer works for the organisation.

https://www.netwerk24.com/netwerk24/nuus/politiek/cmr-sluit-deure-om-druk-op-gauteng-te-plaas-20230425

https://www.netwerk24.com/netwerk24/nuus/aktueel/gesinne-herenig-na-jare-se-gesukkel-20220828

https://www.netwerk24.com/netwerk24/nuus/aktueel/kinderhof-minag-ouers-en-werkers-20220827

https://www.netwerk24.com/netwerk24/nuus/aktueel/ma-hoop-om-met-kinders-herenig-te-word-na-sewe-jaar-20220716

https://www.netwerk24.com/rapport/nuusbriewe/sondag-rapport/hoofstorie/valke-bekyk-cmr-oor-menseroof-20220710-3

https://www.netwerk24.com/netwerk24/nuus/hof/r50-m-eis-teen-ng-welsyn-oor-lolsaak-20220529

https://www.netwerk24.com/netwerk24/nuus/hof/welsyn-rig-kinders-af-in-sekssake-20220515

Looking deeper into all this cases one thing stands out, almost in all cases the same people is involved. From social workers thru to Presiding officers, psychologists, and police officers.

In so many years of children's Advocates fighting against this atrocities no real change happened as of yet. As a matter of fact the situation only gets worse by the day. It can be concluded that either no institution knows the law fully or they are neglecting their duties due to insufficient skills and or places.

As for the general public to disregard a law is no excuse and is not permissible by law enforcement. It's your duty as a citizen to know the law. The same can be applied to all relevant departments.

"In law, ignorantia juris non excusat (Latin for "ignorance of the law excuses not"), or ignorantia legis neminem excusat ("ignorance of law excuses no one"), is a legal principle holding that a person who is unaware of a law may not escape liability for violating that law merely by being unaware of its content."

Chapter 9: In The Words of Robert

" I as a father stood by and watched the love of my life, my children being destroyed by a welfare system. A system who not one day sat down and thought about what they were doing.

They had no connection to my children, they didn't birth them or sat by their beds when they were ill.

They made me out to be this terrible monster who beat his children and neglected them, while I was the only one ever to deeply cared for them. I never beated my children and I never neglected them.

Even when they were in the welfare system I always fought to get them back in my care. I visited them when I was allowed to.

I mourned my children, like a parent losing his children to death. I tried to protect them from all this hurt and pain that was caused by the system. And that's why I ran away with them against the court order. I knew my babies would be damaged when taken away.

To lie down in your bed falling asleep and suddenly wake up because you think you heard your children's laughter, and then realising it's not true is nothing more than psychological torture.

The months I was refused to visit my children was he'll on earth, I did not know if they were OK. I never received calls from them and when I called I was not allowed to speak to them.

I was constantly interrogated by the social workers and everything I did was questioned or investigated.

Everytime just when I thought now I'm going to get my children back, the social worker leaves and a new one is appointed. And everytime the process start all over again with a two year plan that I never saw.

First with Hanna it took sixteen years to get her free from social services. And with my other children seven years.

This cost me my car and all my belongings and all my jobs I was doing to get my children safe.

Over the years of constant stress and trauma I developed Irritable bowl syndrome, high blood pressure, diabetes, kidney failure and heart problems. I also suffer from depression at times that I just need to suppress somehow to cope with everyday living.

Feelings of hurt, anger, rejection overwhelms me at times but I learned to deal with it in my own way.

Today I look at my once beautiful, intelligent, happy children and all I see is traumatised, angry, underdeveloped children.

This will destroy any parents inner core. The worst part is that the organisations and people who caused my children's destruction is still operating.

I sat awake night after night in fear, crying over my lost children. I prayed, I spoke out to numerous institutions and people and no one would help my children or believe me.

The social workers conducted numerous home visits after my kids was removed, they found everything in order. They came with marked vehicles causing the whole neighbourhood to go against me, thinking I'm a terrible parent.

I was alone in this fight and alone in this world fighting a system that didn't want to recognize their mistakes.

Time and time and again I was told by this NPO social workers I cant get my kids. Firstly because I'm a man and I can't take care of girls. Secondly because I have one arm I can't take care of five kids on my own. But yet a lot of single fathers takes care of their daughters. And because I have one arm doesn't make me incompetent to take care of my children. This made me feel useless as a parent. Like I'm no good at all.

I knew the truth but no one heard me. No one cared. I didn't have any documentation to get a lawyer, because a lawyer wants the charges. They can't fight a case without knowing why they are fighting, and I could not provide them with this information as I didn't have it myself.

I felt lost in a world of ugliness and pain. My days would be filled with sorrow even though I cried so much that my tears dried up.

The day Department of Social Development placed my children back in my care was the most wonderful day of my life. It was short-lived though because only then I could see the full impact on my children.

I love my children dearly, I know they have a lot of problems. I can't fix what happened and nor can I take it away. All the hurt and suffering they endured all in the name of money and miss used power.

My words alone can not describe the inner struggles I face and I could only hope that one day my children will know I never gave up on them. I can only pray that this situations gets stopped and that no other family would ever have to go thru this pain and suffering.

It's cruel and inhumane how families are torn apart by entiteties that's supposed to protect them."

Proof of payments made to social services:

STAATSKOERANT, 29 JUNIE 2012 No.35476 3

GOVERNMENT NOTICE

DEPARTMENT OF SOCIAL DEVELOPMENT

No. R. 497 29 June 2012

CHILDREN'S ACT, 2005

AMENDMENT: GENERAL REGULATIONS REGARDING CHILDREN

The Minister of Social Development has, in terms of section 306 of the

Children's Act, 2005 (Act No. 38 of 2005), made the regulations in the

Schedule.

SCHEDULE

1. In these regulations "the Regulations" means the regulations published by

Government Notice No. R.261 of 1 April 2010.

Substitution of regulation 33 of the Regulations

2. Regulation 33 of the Regulations is hereby substituted by the following

regulation:

"Reporting of abuse or deliberate neglect of child

33. (1) A report by a person contemplated in section 110(1) of the Act, who

on reasonable grounds concludes as provided for in that section that a child has been abused in a manner causing physical injury, sexual

abused, emotionally abused or deliberately neglected, must be made to

the provincial department of social development, a designated child

protection organisation or a police official in a form substantially

corresponding to Form 22 by completing that form to the best of that

person's ability and by including in the form such particulars as are

available to him or her.

1) A person authorised by a court order, a designated social worker or a

Police official who removes a child and places such child in temporary safe
Care-

(a) In terms of a children's court order contemplated in section 151 (2) of

The Act; or

(b) Without a court order in terms of section 152(1) of
the Act,

Must complete a form substantially corresponding to Form 36
and submit
It to the temporary safe care with admittance".
Substitution of regulation 1 07 of the Regulations

4. Regulation 1 07 of the Regulations is hereby
substituted by the following

Regulation:
"Fees payable to accredited child protection organisations
107. The following fees, which must be reviewed annually, must
be paid to
An accredited child protection organisation in respect of an
adoption:
SERVICE

(a) Group orientation

MAXIMUM AMOUNT
R275, 00 per session;

(b) Interview/counselling (maximum four sessions)
R275, 00 per hour;

© Home visits (maximum four visits) R440, 00 per hour;

(c) Home study report R550, 00 per report;

€ Court processes R550, 00 per day;
(f) Birth registration R187, 00 per hour;
(g) Administration costs

(h) After-care services

(i) Child study report

R187, 00 per hour;
R550, 00 once-off
Payment; and
R500, 00 per report." (2) A designated child protection organisation or police official to whom a
report contemplated in sub·regulation (1) has been made, must submit
the completed Form 22 to the relevant provincial department of social
development.
(3) The provincial department of social development or designated child
protection organisation to whom a report contemplated in sub·regulation
(1) has been submitted, must submit the particulars of the abuse in a form
identical to Form 23 to the Director-General for inclusion in Part A of the
National Child Protection Register."
Amendment of regulation 40 of the Regulations
Substitution of regulation 1 07 of the Regulations

5. Regulation 1 07 of the Regulations is hereby substituted by the following

Regulation:
"Fees payable to accredited child protection organisations
107. The following fees, which must be reviewed annually, must be paid to

An accredited child protection organisation in respect of an adoption:

SERVICE

(a) Group orientation

MAXIMUM AMOUNT

R275, 00 per session;

(b) Interview/counselling (maximum four sessions) R275, 00 per hour;

© Home visits (maximum four visits) R440, 00 per hour;

(c) Home study report R550, 00 per report;

€ Court processes R550, 00 per day;
(f) Birth registration R187, 00 per hour;
(g) Administration costs
(h) After-care services

(i) Child study report

R187, 00 per hour;
R550, 00 once-off
Payment; and
R500, 00 per report.3. Regulation 40 of the Regulations is hereby amended by the substitution for

paragraph (a) of sub regulation (3) of the following paragraph:

"(a) particulars regarding the date and place of the incident or act that led

to the inclusion of the affected person's name in Part A of the National

Child Protection Register; and".

Amendment of regulation 53 of the Regulations

4. Regulation 53 of the Regulations is hereby amended by the substitution for

sub-regulation (1) of the following sub-regulation:

Chapter 10: Authors Note

This was the story and events of Robert and his family. As the Author of this book it shocking to see that the exact places that is supposed to protect families and children, fails them tremendously.

But the worst part of it all, is that they don't want to correct the mistakes of the past. They rather build on that mistakes or sweep the problems under the carpet.

After intensive investigation over a period of four years, I found that there are more cases like the case of Robert and his family. The stories differ from family to family but the initial removal and the battles are the same. Most of these stories has fabricated documents, allegations without prove, wrong documents and long history of re unification process.

Some of the allegations made towards families, without sufficient proof.

Neglect

Molestation

Abuse.

Some of the cases the allegations started with neglect then changed to abuse and when that failed it was changed to molestation and or rape.

It saddens me to think that someone can come and remove your child, the child you birthed and cared for. To place them in a failing welfare system to be abused, molested, raped, subjected to Satanism, violence and then ultimately be placed on anti psychotic drug because they were traumatised and now experience behavioural problems, mental health conditions.

There are indeed instances where it is really necessary to remove a Child from the family home. However this should be the last resort. The damage within the system is sometimes worse than the occasional slap on the bum from a parent. Parents fighting is not a reason to remove a Child and subject him to the abuse within the system.

Parents not having college funds available and not staying in ten bedroom mansions with flashy cars is not a valid reason to remove a Child.

In South Africa, the unemployment rate is high and most people live from day to day. Is this a reason to remove a Child? And place him in a suffering system that needs to beg society for funding or donations? Why don't the welfare system rather support the families with donations before intervention takes place to remove children?

Should a parent like Margaret be no good for the well being of the children, but another parent like Robert can see to the children's needs, remove the problem parent. Get that parent into rehab or other programs.

We need a change in the welfare system and we need it urgently. A few human rights activists tried to change the way these cases are being handled for the past ten plus years, they made some change but its not enough.

Our Children is the future, if we mess up their life's with trauma, where would it end?

Chapter 11: Documented Meetings

Here is a document of a meeting of the portfolio committee, take note of the highlighted parts.

Children's Amendment Bill: Department of Social Development briefing

Department of Social Development

06 October 2020

Chairperson: Mr M Gungubele (ANC)

Share this page:

Meeting Summary

The Portfolio Committee was briefed by the Department of Social Development on the various clauses of the Children's Amendment Bill [B18 – 2020]. In a virtual meeting, the Department's specialist in legislative drafting and review presented a quarter of the clauses at a time, in a page-by-page fashion, for the Committee's consideration.

Members raised their concern over the Department's capacity to take over the adoption processes from private agencies, as this had the potential to create a backlog in child adoptions, resulting in children languishing in foster care homes and orphanages. The Committee requested that the Department brief them at a later stage on the intended amendments to the adoption processes.

The Children's Court would now deal with cases involving the guardianship of children as a means of alleviating the burden of the High Court. However, the High Court would maintain its jurisdiction to deal with all legal matters in Divorce and guardianship orders.

The Bill was commended by the Committee for making provisions for children with disabilities, such as including a sign language interpreter for children in court. It also commended the Department for updating the Child Protection Register, and the overall rigour which it had shown in dealing with the amendments to the Bill.

Meeting report

The Chairperson asked if the parliamentary advisors and the Departmental legal advisors had convened to discuss whether it would take a comprehensive route in the process of passing the Children's Amendment Bill, or if it would use the foster care provisions only. The Department confirmed that it would go for a comprehensive approach, and estimated that the process would be concluded and referred to the National Council of Provinces (NCOP) by June 2021.

Discussion of clauses 1-15

After Adv Luyanda Mtshotshisa, Specialist: Legislative Drafting and Review, Department of Social Development (DSD), had presented clauses 1-15 of the Bill, Ms B Masango (DA) said that the definition of an orphan seemed to have been amended, and had the potential to be interpreted in multiple ways in clause one. She asked for clarity on the definition. What was the actual age of marriage, as per clause six?

Ms A Abrahams (DA) asked if clause ten gave way for review of the mediation by a court, as it was unclear. Clause 12 stated that a child, if mature, may express its views regarding parental responsibility should parents' divorce—who decides a child's maturity?

Ms D Ngwenya (EFF) asked if any of the clauses made provision for the authorisation of youths being married traditionally, other than being married at the Department of Home Affairs. Clause ten stipulated the rights of fathers if present at the time of conception and/or birth, but did the clause consider reasons for unions being broken, such as the father being a threat to the child and mother's life? Did the clause regarding inter-country adoption consider the potential for children being trafficked?

Response

The current definition of an orphan was when both parents were deceased, according to the current legislation. However, this would be amended to consider one parent being deceased.

The maturity of a child had been determined by common law, such as a child of 16 years old being able to open an insurance policy, and a 14-year-old being able to witness a will, which was common law that was in existence. The Bill sought to determine a set age of maturity.

The prohibition of marriage of children included marriages registered at Home Affairs and traditional marriages. The Children's Act stipulates that no children under the age of 18 years may get married. Previously, guardians were able to grant permission for children under the age of 14 years to get married, but this had been removed from the legislation.

The amendment Bill sought to ensure that families were preferred to any persons who wanted to adopt a child. However, national and inter-country adoptions were still permitted, granted that the prospective adoptive parents meet the requirements as per the Children's Act. The adoption industry was against this amendment, but the DSD continued to pursue this as it was a means of child protection against child trafficking.

The clause pertaining to parental responsibility, where a father was living with the mother at the time of conception and/or birth, came from the approach that the father automatically assumes the responsibility of the child. There were instances where mothers had been raped, and other circumstances where the father had posed a danger to the mother and child, which did not warrant him parental responsibility. In these cases, the courts would have to be engaged in revoking the father's parental responsibility. However, in traditional cases, the father would automatically assume parental responsibility rights.

Follow-up Discussion

The Chairperson asked if the interests of the child would supersede anything at all material times, depending on what was presented to the court? If this was the case, then issues where a child's protection was compromised, the court would revoke rights of parental responsibility. Adv Mtshotshisa confirmed that this was the case.

Ms L Arries (EFF) said that in her community, children were adopted for the wrong reasons and they ended up living in a bad state. The amendment should limit the number of children a person could adopt to ensure that children who were adopted, were taken good care of.

The Chairperson said that the court would always take into account the wellbeing and protection of a child, depending on the information presented to it.

Adv Mtshotshisa concurred with this, stating that the courts and the DSD were aware of persons adopting children for financial gain, hence the preferential adoption by family members.

Discussion of clauses 16-30

Ms Masango asked what matters that were previously handled by the High Court would be referred to the Children's Court. The clause was vague, as it seemed as if only matters pertaining to orphaned and abandoned children would be referred to the Children's Court.

Ms Ngwenya commended the Department for its efforts in being inclusive of disabled children by incorporating sign language in child services. Did the amendments to section 45 mean that people who found abonded children may be granted guardianship while other processes such as foster care were being pursued?

Ms L van der Merwe (IFP) commended the Department for their provisions for disabled children. The amendment of clause 35 provided avenues of recourse for parents who had a child being withheld from them by another parent, and she asked what recourse was available. Were children being limited to the consideration for adoption by family members? Lockdown had resulted in an increase in abandoned children, and in some cases, children had been left on doorsteps, making it difficult to track their biological parents. The approach to limit children to adoption by family members was a negative approach, especially in cases like this.

The Chairperson said that general adoption made in favour of family was problematic, as an abandoned child was often from dysfunctional family dynamics, so this needed to be clarified.

Response

The Amendment Bill was trying to relieve the High Court by referring cases related to children to the Children's Court. However, the High Court would maintain its jurisdiction to deal with any issue.

The Department was not saying that adoption should be done away with. Instead, favour must be given to adoption within families to assist the Department in ensuring child protection. There was often a fine line between adoption and the sale of a child, and the Department was trying to prevent this.

There was no specific recourse in terms of the amendment of Section 35. Recourse would be determined by the parents, and the court would decide if the recourse was just and ideal.

Clause 24, which amended Section 45, did not mean that abandoned children may not be placed in the guardianship of a person that found them. However, the Department was also not saying that just because a person had found a child, that they should keep the child. The determining factor was that the child was being adequately taken care of, and was in a suitable environment.

The Department aimed to have children adopted nationally rather than internationally. Should there be no persons willing to adopt a child nationally, then the child may be adopted internationally. There had been an increase in abandoned children during the lockdown. These children needed to be on the Child Protection Register. There had been 90 children registered during lockdown. The Department was working with non-governmental organizations (NGOs) on intervention plans in this regard.

Discussion of clauses 31-42

Ms Masango asked if the amendment was seeking to grant the Children's Court all guardianship cases or only cases where children had been abandoned. In clause 35, 4A, which sought to amend Section 78, there had been a change in the wording from "must" to "may"—what was the reason for this? She asked for clarity on the existing legislation on adoption which seemed not to be rigorous enough, as the adoption process prioritisation had changed from family being considered first, to national adoption and lastly international adoption.

Ms Abrahams said clause 35 no longer allowed for funding for partial care facilities that partially complied with funding conditionality, and would not include private homes and businesses. How would rural areas be capacitated with this amendment? For example, farmers in rural areas who had facilities would not be eligible for funding, although they were one of the few facilities providing child services to their particular area, but operating from their homes.

Response

Adv Mtshotshisa said that the intention of the amendment bill was that all issues pertaining to children, including guardianship and other matters, would be dealt with by the Children's Court, but the High Court would still deal with these matters as per its constitutional capacity.

There were gaps in the system surrounding adoption. The current acts did not specify that family should be considered first for adoption. There was a fee charged by practitioners for adoptions which was not stipulated in legislature. The Department was concerned that adoption was seen or construed as a business, so it sought to remove fees involved in the adoption process by practitioners and agencies. There was no distinction between adoption and the sale of a child when there were fees involved. The Department was therefore taking over this role as a child protection measure.

Legislation did allow for inter-country adoption, and there was a method to scrutinise such adoptions to prevent children being trafficked. This was an area of adoption where it was difficult to ensure that children were not being trafficked after they had left the borders of South Africa.

Partial care and early childhood development (ECD) facilities were often in the backyard of a house. Once such facilities were funded and the homeowner passed away, the infrastructure may not continue being used for child services, and the funding then went to waste. This was the reason funding of such facilities was currently being contested.

Follow-up Discussion

Ms van der Merwe asked for clarity on whether adoption processes would be done solely by the DSD, to avoid fees charged by agencies. There was an existing crisis in the limited number of social workers, and if the agencies closed down, there was a possibility of children languishing in foster care and orphanages. The fee of about R40 000 charged by agencies were for counselling, social workers and the other support services which were needed. Why did the Department not work with these agencies? The possibility of a backlog of child adoptions could be catastrophic.

Response

Adv Mtshotshisa said that the agencies would not be closed down, but like other welfare services enshrined in the Constitution, it should be free. By charging R40 000, it limited the people that could adopt children.

The Chairperson said that as much as R40 000 may limit the people who were able to utilise adoption agencies, the potential for a backlog in adoptions needed to be considered. Furthermore, the fees charged by agencies were for additional services such as psychologists and social workers, which were essential.

Adv Mtshotshisa said that the Bill did not state that agencies should stop providing services, but sought to take over the services so that adoption was accessible to people who wanted to adopt. NGO's charged a fee for an adoption agreement to be reached, but the Department also subsidised these NGO's. If the Department had money to subsidise NGO's, it could take over the service without taking the rights away from practitioners such as social workers in private practice and lawyers dealing with issues of child adoption.

The Chairperson said that government needed to ensure that the interests of the children at all material times were taken care of. It was thus the government's responsibility to see the realisation of this intention.

Child adoptions that had gone through private agencies were due to the government's lack of capacity to deal with the adoption process. The Department would need to demonstrate that the government had the capacity to deal with this process should the agencies be closed. He suggested that the Department present to the Committee its ability to take over this service fully at a later stage.

Adv Mtshotshisa agreed that a meeting could be arranged to address the Committee on the planned amendments to the adoption processes.

Discussion of clauses 43-60

Ms Abrahams said that there had been a few interactions regarding the placing of Early Childhood Development – ECD, in the portfolio of the Department of Basic Education (DBE), and requested that this be work-shopped outside of this meeting. The Children's Amendment Bill had been costly to pass, and there was uncertainty of how it would fit in with the migration to the DBE and what it would mean for school curricula. During lockdown, the ECD sector had stated that what worked in affluent areas did not necessarily work in townships and rural areas—did the new legislation properly address this? It was concerning that this sector had not been included when the Bill went out for public comment. Clause 48 introduced the word "protection" in the amendment to section 94. Why was the word "nutrition" not included, considering that it was a part of the Department's funding policy?

The Chairperson asked Ms Abrahams if there was a distinction between protection and nutrition. She said that was the clarity she was seeking, as the clause was adding "protection" to the wording, whereas it already stated that "security" was part of the wording. Was there a distinction between protection and security?

Ms Ngwenya said that there were already many ECDs that were not registered, and this needed to be looked into. The proposed new procedures and requirements for ECD centres to be registered should not result in more ECD centres going unregistered, as this would take the DSD many steps back. Monitoring and evaluation within the DSD district offices was necessary to curb fraudulent activities of the personnel overlooking processes when registering ECD centres.

According to clauses 52 and 53, the Member of the Executive Council (MEC) for Social Development may assign the performance of some or all of the functions to a municipal manager, and to effect minor consequential amendments. This may be problematic, as municipalities did not perform as expected.

Would municipalities be able to adhere to this new clause, considering the current state of municipal management? Would this result in more corruption within Early Childhood Development centres?

Response

Adv Mtshotshisa said that the differences in ECD needs between affluent areas compared to townships and rural areas could be dealt with in greater depth in the Bill. The ECD sector had not been included for comment during the public participation process, but this was an incidental matter and more administrative, rather than substantive. The clauses pertaining to ECD centres were not introducing anything new. The registering of an ECD centre was the same as registering a partial care facility, and thus more administrative than substantive.

The Department's belief was that nutrition was included in the term 'protection'. If a child was suffering from famine, the child was not protected, so nutrition went hand-in-hand with protection. If the Committee preferred "nutrition" to be explicitly stated, then this could be added.

Clause 46 sought to amend section 92, which were requirements for ECDs. The requirements had already been in effect, so it was not creating any burden for ECD applicants. The DSD was not a stumbling block for facilities being registering, but the mushrooming of illegal facilities was an issue. This issue usually lay with municipalities and the expectations of their role.

The issues of fraud that may ensue due to the registration of ECDs was because they were multi-sectoral in nature. People wanted to comply with registration, as seen by the amount of applications which the Department had received, but they got frustrated by all the red tape. For instance, there were municipalities that took about three years for rezoning certificates to be finalized, and it could cost between R60 000 and R100 000.

If these requirements were changed, then the lives of children were being risked, as the buildings of ECD centres may not comply with the building regulations and other bylaws of municipalities.

Discussion of clauses 61-90

Ms Masango asked for clarity on clause 82.

Ms van der Merwe said that clauses pertaining to the National Child Protection Register, which dealt with persons unsuitable to work with children, were commendable. In the past, people complained that the register was not up to date. Once it had been updated, what would compel employers, schools and ECDs to check that employees were not on this register? Would there be consequences for employers that were found to have employees working with children, but were not on the register?

Response

Adv Mtshotshisa said that clause 82, which sought to amend section 150, aimed to deal with comprehensive legal solutions and giving clarity on abandoned children and those who should take care of these children. This provision had extended the current clause to include a register of children who had have been victims of trafficking, and were unaccompanied from a migrant country.

He agreed that employers who did not check employees against the register needed to be penalised. There needed to be a stipulated timeframe for when employers should recheck their employees against the register to ensure that they had not been newly added to the register.

Discussion of clauses 96-119

Ms Masango asked for clarity on the intended amendments to Section 234.

Response

Adv Mtshotshisa stated that the amendment would add "or a family member" to the current list which regulated post-adoption agreements.

Discussion of clauses 120-150

Ms Masango asked for confirmation that there would be a discussion that would pertain to adoptions. She also requested that a breakdown be provided of the R32 billion to be spent on ECDs, as per the memorandum of the Bill.

Response

Mr Linton Mchunu, Acting Director-General, DSD, stated that the query regarding the memorandum would be followed up, and the Department would brief the Committee on the various questions that had arisen surrounding the adoption processes.

The meeting was adjourned.

Chapter 12 Case of Helen

Helen was a young mother who was caught up in a marriage of abuse, her husband was addicted to drugs and alcohol. Helen had a baby of six months old a little girl called Megan.

One evening Helen and her husband drove to a restaurant to have a drink, from there they wanted to go to another restaurant for dinner.

Megan was in the car in the back when a smash and grab incident occurred. Helen took Megan and ran to another car where a woman offered help and took Helen with Megan to the police station.

Helen opened a case for the smash and grab and she called her father as she didn't have her house keys or anything. Her father offered to take care of Megan for the evening so Helen could have a chance to get all this sorted out.

The next day friends of Helens father who she knew offered that Megan stay with them for a few days and Helen agreed. She wanted the best for Megan and she knew that her current husband was no good.

When Helen went to get Megan after a few days she was told that Social services placed Megan in the care of that people with a form 36. Megan was placed in Foster care for two years without Helen being present.

The foster parents and the social worker wanted Helen to sign documents so they could get a passport to take Megan out of he country on holiday. Helen refused to sign that documents.

However Helen soon found out that a false passport and birth certificate was used where they changed Megan's surname to take her on holiday outside of South Africa. She also found out that her daughter was enrolled in school with this fake birth certificate.

On this case there are many inconsistencies, but because the case is not solved yet after eleven years, not to much can be said as it is a ongoing court case.

What can be said is that again a form 36 illegal document was used. The mother was not taken to court within twenty four hours after removal. And false documents was used to take Megan Cross country. The foster care placement was again overseen till the child turns eighteen, without the mother being present. The child has no knowledge about her mother and she has no idea that the surname she is using is fake and not her real surname. The last visitation with her child was when Megan was about five years old she is currently twelve years old.

Helen turned her life around, she divorced her husband, she stopped using drugs, she went for parental classes, she had a secure job and a place to stay. Random drug tests was performed on her to make sure she is clean. She furthered her studies. But still social services refused to re unify her daughter.

Taking into consideration that the child was removed from Helen when only six months old with no knowledge about her biological mother. No proper visitations or any contact, it would be difficult to re unify her.

Helens parental rights was not absconded by court.

The best way to remedy this situation would be to start supervised visitations between mother and daughter. To start building a bond and relationship, getting to know each other.

Chapter 13: Conclusion

Thru the proof of Robert and Helens cases, we can see that urgent change is necessary to protect the most vulnerable in our society.

Also note that not all cases are illegal and unsubstantiated. The current problem areas include but is not limited to:

1. **Properly qualified social workers as stipulated in the following document.**

DEPARTMENT OF SOCIAL DEVELOPMENT

Social Service Professions Act 110, 1978

RULES RELATING TO THE QUALIFICATIONS FOR Re Registration AS A SOCIAL

AUXILIARY WORKER

In terms of section 18(2) of the Social Service Professions Act, 1978 (Act 11 0 of 1978) as

Amended, the South African Council for Social Service Professions hereby makes the rules set

Out in the Schedule hereto.

SCHEDULE

DEFINITIONS

1 In these Rules "the Act" means the Social Service Professions Act, 1978 (Act 110 of 1978),

And any expression to which a meaning has been assigned in the Act shall have such

Meaning and, unless the context otherwise indicates-

"chairperson of the board" means the chairperson appointed by the Minister in terms of

Regulation 4 of the regulations regarding the functioning of professional boards.

"National Qualifications Framework (1\IQF)" means a comprehensive system approved by the

Minister of Education for the classification, registration, publication and articulation of quality assured national qualifications.

"prescribed" means with regard to fees as prescribed by regulation 28 in terms of the Social

Service Professions Act, 1978, as amended.

"presidenf' means the president of the South African Council for Social Service Professions.

"provider" means for the purposes of these regulations, a recognized and accredited body that

Delivers learning programmes focused on the achievement of specified 1\IQF registered

Qualifications and standards on the South African Qualifications Authority's (SAQA) database

And manages the assessment of learning achievements or prior to the existence of SAQA a

Body recognized by the Council for this purpose.

"qualification" means a qualification registered by the South African Qualifications Authority, or

Prior to its existence recognized by the SACSSP.

"Recognition of prior learning (RPL)" means an act by a provider comprising the comparison

With the previous learning and experience of a learner howsoever obtained against the

Learning outcomes acquired for a specified qualification and the acceptance for purposes of

Qualification of that which meets the requirements.

Social Auxiliary Work" means an act or activity practiced by a social auxiliary worker under the

.. guidance and control of a social worker and as a supporting service to a social worker to

Achieve the aims of social work.

"Social Auxiliary Worker" means a person practicing social auxiliary work and registered under

Section 18 of the Act.

"Student social auxiliary worker" means a person who is registered with the SACSSP on

Condition that he or she completes the necessary qualification in order to meet the

Requirements for registration.

QUALIFICATIONS FOR REGISTRATION

1. (1)The following qualifications are prescribed for the purposes of section 18(1) of the

Act:

a. A Further Education and Training (FET) Certificate in Social Auxiliary Work equivalent to

An NQF Level 4 qualification registered with the South African Qualifications Authority;

Or

a. A Certificate in Social Auxiliary Work which the Council awarded to a person who

Successfully completed the study course in Social Auxiliary Work offered by the

SACSSP and in respect of which the holder of the qualification was enrolled for such

Qualification before 30 June 2006 or received written approval by the Council for

Enrolment at a later date as determined by the Council; or

(c) A qualification obtained after completion of a learning programme at a provider which

The Council regards as equal to or higher than the qualification referred to in sub rule

(a); or

a. Theoretical and/or experiential learning approved by the Council equivalent to the

Qualification referred to in sub rule (a): Provided that the applicant submit a portfolio of

Evidence, which may include an assessment, proving that the candidate meets the

Outcomes reflected in the FET Certificate in Social Auxiliary Work referred to in sub rule

(a) Or

€ Proof from a provider that the candidate successfully completed both the theoretical and

Practical learning of two year courses in the subject Social Work, with a recognized

Provider.

(2) The qualifications referred to in sub rule (1) may be obtained partially or as a whole

Through RPL.

(3) The SACSSP may, on the completion of a short course recognized by the SACSSP for

This purpose, register a social auxiliary worker in a particular field of practice and specify

The conditions for such practice

REPEAL OF RULES

1. The Rules made under the Social Work Act, 1978, published as Board Notice 135 in

Government Gazette 13620 of 15 November 1991, as amended by Board Notices 66 in

Government Gazette 14900 of 2 July 1993, 72 in Government Gazette 14967 of 16 July

1993, 4 in Government Gazette 15420 of 14 January 1994, 29 in Government Gazette

16495 of 30 June 1995 and 54 in Government Gazette 21396 of 28 July 2000 are

Hereby repealed.

COMMENCEMENT

1. These rules shall come into operation on the date of the publication thereof

1. **Department of Social Development to employ more**

accredited social workers to attend to field work. And be the only body that can remove a Child when the need arise with the correct documentation namely Form 22.

When is a Form 22 used?

According to section 150 of the children's act the following circumstances describe children in need of care and protection. A child who:

- has been abandoned or orphaned and is without any visible means of support;

-

- displays behaviour which cannot be controlled by the parent or care-giver;
- lives or works on the streets or begs for a living;
- is addicted to a dependence-producing substance and is without any support to obtain treatment for such dependency;
- has been exploited or lives in circumstances that expose the child to exploitation;
- lives in or is exposed to circumstances which may seriously harm that child's physical, mental or social well-being;
- may be at risk if returned to the custody of the parent, guardian or care-giver of the child as there is reason to believe that he or she will live in or be exposed to circumstances which may seriously harm the physical, mental or social well-being of the child;
- is in a state of physical or mental neglect; or

- is being maltreated, abused, deliberately neglected or degraded by a parent, a care-giver, a person who has parental responsibilities and rights or a family member of the child or by a person under whose control the child is.

1. Department SOCIAL Development take more action against unregistered places of safety, and remove children from this places.

1. Department of Social Development to assist parents who's children was illegally removed with re unification. This must be done in a case by case manner. Not all cases are the same. Proper investigation must be done. To just re unify left right and centre you might end up giving kids to parents who really were not good.

1. Employ "watchdogs" to do random visits at Children's Homes, Places of safety and Secure Care centres to do quality checks.

1. Police officials must be trained to deal with the mental health act and children clashing with the law.

1. Support systems must be put in place for families that went thru years of trauma because of a failing system.

1. More facilitaties should be available for minors with behavioural problems. With trained professionals who can assist the children in emotional regulation and trauma.

1. The timeframe for criminal capacity evaluation should be nothing more than 30 days to reduce unnecessary stress to

the minor.

1. Minors should not be handcuffed when taken to court. Its humiliating and traumatic.

1. Human Rights Activists should be involved in making decisions to amendments in the children's act.

1. When the public reports abuse at Childcare facilitaties it should be investigated immediately and a full report should be made available.

1. A more constructive way needs to be looked at to accommodate children with mental illness and or behavioural problems that causes instability. There is not enough mental institutions in Provinces. The 72 hour observation in a normal state facility is not sufficient to care.

1. Children's courts should be more family friendly and give the parents a chance to state their case.

1. Children's courts should also make sure the social workers recommendation of placement is safe and registered.

1. Parents must be in court when a judgement to take away their children is made, and that court order should be available to the parent.

Chapter 14: Poems for Families

Silent Cries

In the quiet of the night, echoes of despair, Families torn apart, a pain too deep to bear. Children taken from loving arms, unjustly so, A wound that time struggles to heal, a sorrow that grows.

Innocent laughter replaced by silent cries, Parents left questioning, under tear-filled skies. The warmth of home now a distant dream, Shattered by a system's cold, relentless scheme.

Hearts once full of joy, now heavy with grief, Seeking answers, justice, and a moment of relief. Memories of small hands, held tight in the past, Now linger as shadows, in a world so vast.

Yet, amidst the darkness, a flicker of light, Families united, ready to fight. For every tear shed, a promise is made, To stand strong, undeterred, never to fade.

In the face of injustice, they find their voice, Demanding change, for they have no choice. For the love of their children, they rise above, A testament to the power of unwavering love.

The Child's Voice

Whispers of Innocence

In a world so big, I felt so small,

Taken from my home, my heart, my all.

False words were spoken, and shadows grew,

In the halls of strangers, I found no clue.

They said I was unsafe, they said I was lost,

But the truth was twisted, at such a cost.

My tears fell silent, my voice unheard,

In a place where love was just a word.

Each night I dream of a place called home,

Where laughter echoes, and I'm not alone.

But here I am, in this cold, strange bed,

With memories of warmth dancing in my head.

I miss the hugs, the familiar scent,

The love that was real, the time we spent.

Now fear is my friend, and pain my guide,

In this world where I must hide.

But deep inside, a spark remains,

A hope that one day, I'll break these chains.

For truth has a way of finding light,

And love will guide me through the night.

So I hold on tight, to dreams so dear,

That one day soon, I'll conquer this fear.

And in the arms of those I trust,

I'll find my way, because I must.

Chapter 15 From the heart of the Author

Writing this book and looking at all the evidence was one of the hardest things I ever had to do.

With every piece of information I wrote I had mixed emotions, from a deep sadness to a anger that build up. I cried and I had sleepless nights.

I can only but imagine the pain and the torture some of the families endured at the hands of those that was supposed to protect them.

I spoke to several people who went thru this types of removals, all this stories is nothing more than horrific. I only used two cases in this edition because each story is so significant that the book will never end.

The psychological damage to this children is severe and the chances of them ever living a normal life is slim. They were severely traumatised and it had long term effects.

During this investigations I found that numerous emails and petitions against this types of cases was done, to no avail.

The only thing I as the author can hope and pray for is that justice would be served on those who caused this severe pain.

I can only but hope and pray that one day the light will overshadow the dark in our society. That every person would take responsibility for their actions and fix what they have broken.

Dedications

Firstly I want to thank all the families who spoke to me about their painful experiences, I know it was very hard.

Thank you to some human rights activists that gave me some information into the law.

Thank you to the social workers who really do care and do a great job. The ones that's not there for a salary but because they have a passion for families.

I also want to say, The parents who couldn't take the abuse and hurt and humiliation anymore, the ones who committed suicide or decided to just disappear, you were a good parent. The hurt got to much to handle and you felt you had nothing more to give or to lose.

I hereby close off this book, there will be other editions. Look out for them.

May the Lord always guide you and protect you against all evil for sometimes its unseen.

Signed by: Natashia Roberts

Especially for Ramona Niemand

Don't miss out!

Visit the website below and you can sign up to receive emails whenever Natashia Roberts publishes a new book. There's no charge and no obligation.

https://books2read.com/r/B-A-LEEBC-YBYYE

Connecting independent readers to independent writers.

About the Author

Hi my name is Natashia, a mother of 2. I love writing and researching difficult topics. My passion for children made me write books especially for them to help them learn. I hope you find my books helpful.